D1065321

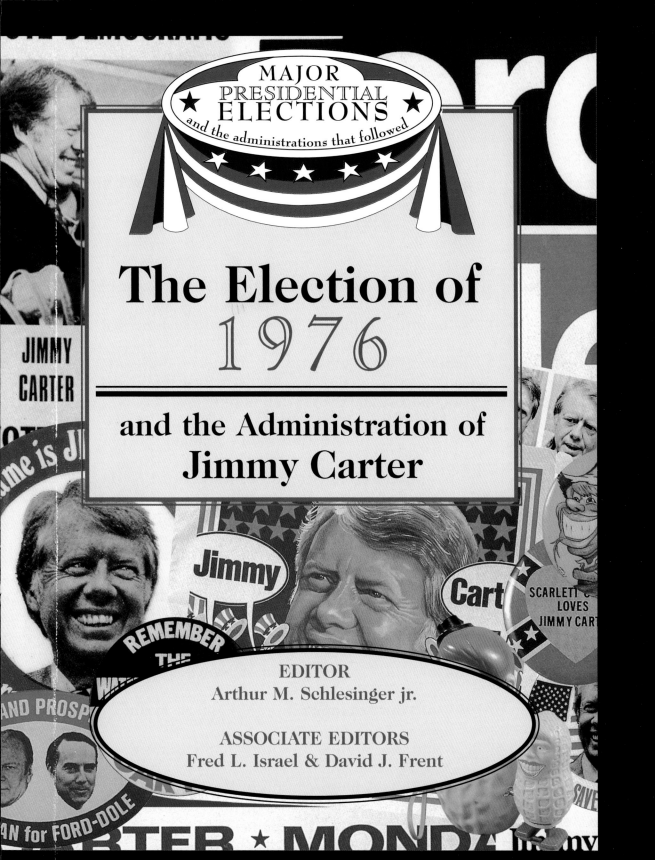

MAJOR PRESIDENTIAL ELECTIONS
and the administrations that followed

The Election of
1976

and the Administration of
Jimmy Carter

EDITOR
Arthur M. Schlesinger jr.

ASSOCIATE EDITORS
Fred L. Israel & David J. Frent

The Elections of 1789 & 1792 and the Administration of George Washington

The Election of 1800 and the Administration of Thomas Jefferson

The Election of 1828 and the Administration of Andrew Jackson

The Election of 1840 and the Harrison/Tyler Administrations

The Election of 1860 and the Administration of Abraham Lincoln

The Election of 1876 and the Administration of Rutherford B. Hayes

The Election of 1896 and the Administration of William McKinley

The Election of 1912 and the Administration of Woodrow Wilson

The Election of 1932 and the Administration of Franklin D. Roosevelt

The Election of 1948 and the Administration of Harry S. Truman

The Election of 1960 and the Administration of John F. Kennedy

The Election of 1968 and the Administration of Richard Nixon

The Election of 1976 and the Administration of Jimmy Carter

The Election of 1980 and the Administration of Ronald Reagan

The Election of 2000 and the Administration of George W. Bush

The Election of
1976

and the Administration of Jimmy Carter

EDITOR

Arthur M. Schlesinger, jr.
Albert Schweitzer Chair in the Humanities
The City University of New York

ASSOCIATE EDITORS

Fred L. Israel
Department of History
The City College of New York

David J. Frent
The David J. and Janice L. Frent
Political Americana Collection

Mason Crest Publishers
Philadelphia

Produced by OTTN Publishing, Stockton, New Jersey

Mason Crest Publishers
370 Reed Road
Broomall PA 19008
www.masoncrest.com

Research Consultant: Patrick R. Hilferty
Editorial Assistant: Jane Ziff

First printing

1 3 5 7 9 8 6 4 2

Library of Congress Cataloging-in-Publication Data

The election of 1976 and the administration of Jimmy Carter / editor, Arthur M. Schlesinger, Jr.;
associate editors, Fred L. Israel & David J. Frent.
      p. cm. — (Major presidential elections and the administrations that followed)
Summary: A discussion of the presidential election of 1976 and the subsequent administration
of Jimmy Carter, based on source documents.
   Includes bibliographical references and index.
   ISBN 1-59084-363-0
1. Presidents—United States—Election—1976—Juvenile literature. 2. Presidents—United
States—Election—1976—Sources—Juvenile literature 3. Carter, Jimmy, 1924—-Juvenile
literature. 4. United States—Politics and government—1977-1981—Juvenile literature.
5. United States—Politics and government—1977-1981—Sources—Juvenile literature.
[1. Presidents—Election—1976—Sources. 2. Carter, Jimmy, 1924- 3. Elections. 4. United
States—Politics and government—1977-1981—Sources.]
I. Schlesinger, Arthur Meier, 1917- II. Israel, Fred L. III. Frent, David J. IV. Series.
E868 .E44 2002
324.973'0925—dc21

                                                                                    2002011773

**Publisher's note: all quotations in this book come
from original sources, and contain the spelling and
grammatical inconsistencies of the original text.**

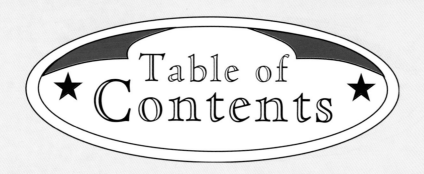

Table of Contents

★ INTRODUCTION ★
Arthur M. Schlesinger, Jr.

America suffers from a sort of intermittent fever—what one may call a quintan ague. Every fourth year there come terrible shakings, passing into the hot fit of the presidential election; then follows what physicians call "the interval"; then again the fit.

—James Bryce, *The American Commonwealth* (1888)

Running for president is the central rite in the American political order. It was not always so. *Choosing* the chief magistrate had been the point of the quadrennial election from the beginning, but it took a long while for candidates to *run* for the highest office in the land; that is, to solicit, visibly and actively, the support of the voters. These volumes show through text and illustration how those aspiring to the White House have moved on from ascetic self-restraint to shameless self-merchandising. This work thereby illuminates the changing ways the American people have conceived the role of their President. I hope it will also recall to new generations some of the more picturesque and endearing dimensions of American politics.

The primary force behind the revolution in campaign attitudes and techniques was a development unforeseen by the men who framed the Constitution—the rise of the party system. Party competition was not at all their original intent. Quite the contrary: inspired at one or two removes by Lord Bolingbroke's British tract of half a century earlier, *The Idea of a Patriot King*, the Founding Fathers envisaged a Patriot President, standing above party and faction, representing the whole people, offering the nation nonpartisan leadership virtuously dedicated to the common good.

The ideal of the Patriot President was endangered, the Founding Fathers believed, by twin menaces—factionalism and factionalism's ugly offspring, the demagogue. Party competition would only encourage unscrupulous men to appeal to popular passion and prejudice. Alexander Hamilton in the 71st Federalist bemoaned the plight of the people, "beset as they continually are . . . by the snares of the ambitious, the avaricious, the desperate, by the artifices of men who possess their confidence more than they deserve it, and of those who seek to possess rather than to deserve it."

Pervading the Federalist was a theme sounded explicitly both in the first paper and the last: the fear that unleashing popular passions would bring on "the military despotism of a victorious demagogue." If the "mischiefs of faction" were, James Madison admitted in the Tenth Federalist, "sown in the nature of man," the object of politics was to repress this insidious disposition, not to yield to it. "If I could not go to heaven but with a party," said Thomas Jefferson, "I would not go there at all."

So the Father of his Country in his Farewell Address solemnly warned his countrymen against "the baneful effects of the spirit of party." That spirit, Washington conceded, was "inseparable from our nature"; but for popular government it was "truly their worst enemy." The "alternate domination of one faction over another," Washington said, would lead in the end to "formal and permanent despotism." The spirit of a party, "a fire not to be quenched . . . demands a uniform vigilance to prevent its bursting into a flame, lest, instead of warming, it should consume."

Yet even as Washington called on Americans to "discourage and restrain" the spirit of party, parties were beginning to crystallize around him. The eruption of partisanship in defiance of such august counsel argued that party competition might well serve functional necessities in the democratic republic.

After all, honest disagreement over policy and principle called for candid debate. And parties, it appeared, had vital roles to play in the consummation of the Constitution. The distribution of powers among three equal branches inclined the national government toward a chronic condition of stalemate. Parties offered the means of overcoming the constitutional separation of powers by coordinating the executive and legislative branches and furnishing the connective tissue essential to effective government. As national associations, moreover, parties were a force against provincialism and separatism. As instruments of compromise, they encouraged, within the parties as well as between them, the containment and mediation of national quarrels, at least until slavery broke the parties up. Henry D. Thoreau cared little enough for politics, but he saw the point: "Politics is, as it were, the gizzard of society, full of grit and gravel, and the two political parties are its two opposite halves, which grind on each other."

Furthermore, as the illustrations in these volumes so gloriously remind us, party competition was a great source of entertainment and fun—all the more important in those faraway days before the advent of baseball and football, of movies and radio and television. "To take a hand in the regulation of society and to discuss it," Alexis de Tocqueville observed when he visited America in the 1830s, "is his biggest concern and, so to speak, the only pleasure an American knows. . . . Even the women frequently attend public meetings and listen to political harangues as a recreation from their household labors. Debating clubs are, to a certain extent, a substitute for theatrical entertainments."

Condemned by the Founding Fathers, unknown to the Constitution, parties nonetheless imperiously forced themselves into political life. But the party system rose from the bottom up. For half a century, the first half-dozen Presidents continued to hold themselves above party. The disappearance of the Federalist Party after the War of 1812 suspended party competition. James Monroe, with no opponent at all in the election of 1820, presided proudly over the Era of Good Feelings, so called because there were no parties around to excite ill feelings. Monroe's successor, John Quincy Adams, despised electioneering and inveighed against the "fashion of peddling for popularity by traveling around the country gathering crowds together, hawking for public dinners, and spouting empty speeches." Men of the old republic believed presidential candidates should be men who already deserved the people's confidence rather than those seeking to win it. Character and virtue, not charisma and ambition, should be the grounds for choosing a President.

Adams was the last of the old school. Andrew Jackson, by beating him in the 1828 election, legitimized party politics and opened a new political era. The rationale of the new school was provided by Jackson's counselor and successor, Martin Van Buren, the classic philosopher of the role of party in the American democracy. By the time Van Buren took his own oath of office in 1837, parties were entrenched as the instruments of American self-government. In Van Buren's words, party battles "rouse the sluggish to exertion, give increased energy to the most active intellect, excite a salutary vigilance over our public functionaries, and prevent that apathy which has proved the ruin of Republics."

Apathy may indeed have proved the ruin of republics, but rousing the sluggish to exertion proved, ironically, the ruin of Van Buren. The architect of the party system became the first casualty of the razzle-dazzle campaigning the system quickly generated. The Whigs' Tippecanoe-and-Tyler-too campaign of 1840 transmuted the democratic Van Buren into a gilded aristocrat and assured his defeat at the polls. The "peddling for popularity" John Quincy Adams had deplored now became standard for party campaigners.

But the new methods were still forbidden to the presidential candidates themselves. The feeling lingered from earlier days that stumping the country in search of votes was demagoguery beneath the dignity of the presidency. Van Buren's code permitted—indeed expected—parties to inscribe their creed in plat-forms and candidates to declare their principles in letters published in news-papers. Occasionally candidates—William Henry Harrison in 1840, Winfield Scott in 1852—made a speech, but party surrogates did most of the hard work.

As late as 1858, Van Buren, advising his son John, one of the great popular orators of the time, on the best way to make it to the White House, emphasized the "rule . . . that the people will never make a man President who is so importunate as to show by his life and conversation that he not only has an eye on, but is in active pursuit of the office. . . . No man who has laid himself out for it, and was unwise enough to let the people into his secret, ever yet obtained it. Clay, Calhoun, Webster, Scott, and a host of lesser lights, should serve as a guide-post to future aspirants."

The continuing constraint on personal campaigning by candidates was reinforced by the desire of party managers to present their nominees as all things to all men. In 1835 Nicholas Biddle, the wealthy Philadelphian who had been Jackson's mortal opponent in the famous Bank War, advised the Whigs not to let General Harrison "say one single word about his principles or his creed. . . . Let him say nothing, promise nothing. Let no committee, no convention, no town meeting ever extract from him a single word about what he thinks now, or what he will do hereafter. Let the use of pen and ink be wholly forbidden as if he were a mad poet in Bedlam."

We cherish the memory of the famous debates in 1858 between Abraham Lincoln and Stephen A. Douglas. But those debates were not part of a presidential election. When the presidency was at stake two years later, Lincoln gave no campaign speeches on the issues darkly dividing the country. He even expressed doubt about party platforms—"the formal written platform system," as he called it. The candidate's character and record, Lincoln thought, should constitute his platform: "On just such platforms all our earlier and better Presidents were elected."

However, Douglas, Lincoln's leading opponent in 1860, foreshadowed the future when he broke the sound barrier and dared venture forth on thinly disguised campaign tours. Yet Douglas established no immediate precedent. Indeed, half a dozen years later Lincoln's successor, Andrew Johnson, discredited presidential stumping by his "swing around the circle" in the midterm election of 1866. "His performances in a western tour in advocacy of his own election," commented Benjamin F. Butler, who later led the fight in Congress for Johnson's impeachment, ". . . disgusted everybody." The tenth article of impeachment charged Johnson with bringing "the high office of the President of the United States into contempt, ridicule, and disgrace" by delivering "with a loud voice certain intemperate, inflammatory, and scandalous harangues . . . peculiarly indecent and unbecoming in the Chief Magistrate of the United States."

Though presidential candidates Horatio Seymour in 1868, Rutherford B. Hayes in 1876, and James A. Garfield in 1880 made occasional speeches, only Horace Greeley in 1872, James G. Blaine in 1884, and most spectacularly, William Jennings Bryan in 1896 followed Douglas's audacious example of stumping the country. Such tactics continued to provoke disapproval. Bryan, said John Hay, who had been Lincoln's private secretary and was soon to become McKinley's secretary of state, "is begging for the presidency as a tramp might beg for a pie."

Respectable opinion still preferred the "front porch" campaign, employed by Garfield, by Benjamin Harrison in 1888, and most notably by McKinley in 1896. Here candidates received and addressed numerous delegations at their own homes—a form, as the historian Gil Troy writes, of "stumping in place."

While candidates generally continued to stand on their dignity, popular campaigning in presidential elections flourished in these years, attaining new heights of participation (82 percent of eligible voters in 1876 and never once from 1860 to 1900 under 70 percent) and new wonders of pyrotechnics and ballyhoo. Parties mobilized the electorate as never before, and political iconography was never more ingenious and fantastic. "Politics, considered not as the science of government, but as the art of winning elections and securing office," wrote the keen British observer James Bryce, "has reached in the United States a development surpassing in elaborateness that of England or France as much as the methods of those countries surpass the methods of

Servia or Roumania." Bryce marveled at the "military discipline" of the parties, at "the demonstrations, the parades and receptions, the badges and brass bands and triumphal arches," at the excitement stirred by elections—and at "the disproportion that strikes a European between the merits of the presidential candidate and the blazing enthusiasm which he evokes."

Still the old taboo held back the presidential candidates themselves. Even so irrepressible a campaigner as President Theodore Roosevelt felt obliged to hold his tongue when he ran for reelection in 1904. This unwonted abstinence reminded him, he wrote in considerable frustration, of the July day in 1898 when he was "lying still under shell fire" during the Spanish-American War. "I have continually wished that I could be on the stump myself."

No such constraint inhibited TR, however, when he ran again for the presidency in 1912. Meanwhile, and for the first time, *both* candidates in 1908—Bryan again, and William Howard Taft—actively campaigned for the prize. The duties of the office, on top of the new requirements of campaigning, led Woodrow Wilson to reflect that same year, four years before he himself ran for President, "Men of ordinary physique and discretion cannot be Presidents and live, if the strain be not somehow relieved. We shall be obliged always to be picking our chief magistrates from among wise and prudent athletes,—a small class."

Theodore Roosevelt and Woodrow Wilson combined to legitimate a new conception of presidential candidates as active molders of public opinion in active pursuit of the highest office. Once in the White House, Wilson revived the custom, abandoned by Jefferson, of delivering annual state of the union addresses to Congress in person. In 1916 he became the first incumbent President to stump for his own reelection.

The activist candidate and the bully-pulpit presidency were expressions of the growing democratization of politics. New forms of communication were reconfiguring presidential campaigns. In the nineteenth century the press, far more fiercely partisan then than today, had been the main carrier of political information. In the twentieth century the spread of advertising techniques and the rise of the electronic media—radio, television, computerized public opinion polling—wrought drastic changes in the methodology of politics. In particular the electronic age diminished and now threatens to dissolve the historic role of the party.

The old system had three tiers: the politician at one end; the voter at the other; and the party in between. The party's function was to negotiate between the politician and the voters, interpreting each to the other and providing the link that held the political process together. The electric revolution has substantially abolished the sovereignty of the party. Where once the voter turned to the local party leader to find out whom to support, now he looks at television and makes up his own mind. Where once the politician turned to the local party leader to find out what people are thinking, he now takes a computerized poll.

The electronic era has created a new breed of professional consultants, "handlers," who by the 1980s had taken control of campaigns away from the politicians. The traditional pageantry—rallies, torchlight processions, volunteers, leaflets, billboards, bumper stickers—is now largely a thing of the past. Television replaces the party as the means of mobilizing the voter. And as the party is left to wither on the vine, the presidential candidate becomes more pivotal than ever. We shall see the rise of personalist movements, founded not on historic organizations but on compelling personalities, private fortunes, and popular frustrations. Without the stabilizing influence of parties, American politics would grow angrier, wilder, and more irresponsible.

Things have changed considerably from the austerities of the old republic. Where once voters preferred to call presumably reluctant candidates to the duties of the supreme magistracy and rejected pursuit of the office as evidence of dangerous ambition, now they expect candidates to come to them, explain their views and plead for their support. Where nonpartisan virtue had been the essence, now candidates must prove to voters that they have the requisite "fire in the belly." "'Twud be inth'restin," said Mr. Dooley, ". . . if th' fathers iv th' counthry cud come back an' see what has happened while they've been away. In times past whin ye voted f'r prisident ye didn't vote f'r a man. Ye voted f'r a kind iv a statue that ye'd put up in ye'er own mind on a marble pidistal. Ye nivir heerd iv George Wash'nton goin' around th' counthry distributin' five cint see-gars."

We have reversed the original notion that ambition must be disguised and the office seek the man. Now the man—and soon, one must hope, the woman— seeks the office and does so without guilt or shame or inhibition. This is not necessarily a degradation of democracy. Dropping the disguise is a gain for candor, and personal avowals of convictions and policies may elevate and educate the electorate.

On the other hand, the electronic era has dismally reduced both the intellectual content of campaigns and the attention span of audiences. In the nineteenth century political speeches lasted for a couple of hours and dealt with issues in systematic and exhaustive fashion. Voters drove wagons for miles to hear Webster and Clay, Bryan and Teddy Roosevelt, and felt cheated if the famous orator did not give them their money's worth. Then radio came along and cut political addresses down first to an hour, soon to thirty minutes—still enough time to develop substantive arguments.

But television has shrunk the political talk first to fifteen minutes, now to the sound bite and the thirty-second spot. Advertising agencies today sell candidates with all the cynical contrivance they previously devoted to selling detergents and mouthwash. The result is the debasement of American politics. "The idea that you can merchandise candidates for high office like breakfast cereal," Adlai Stevenson said in 1952, "is the ultimate indignity to the democratic process."

Still Bryce's "intermittent fever" will be upon us every fourth year. We will continue to watch wise if not always prudent athletes in their sprint for the White House, enjoy the quadrennial spectacle and agonize about the outcome.

"The strife of the election," said Lincoln after his reelection in 1864, "is but human-nature practically applied to the facts. What has occurred in this case, must ever recur in similar cases. Human-nature will not change."

Lincoln, as usual, was right. Despite the transformation in political methods there remains a basic continuity in political emotions. "For a long while before the appointed time has come," Tocqueville wrote more than a century and a half ago, "the election becomes the important and, so to speak, the all-engrossing topic of discussion. Factional ardor is redoubled, and all the artificial passions which the imagination can create in a happy and peaceful land are agitated and brought to light. . . .

"As the election draws near, the activity of intrigue and the agitation of the populace increase; the citizens are divided into hostile camps, each of which assumes the name of its favorite candidate; the whole nation glows with feverish excitement; the election is the daily theme of the press, the subject of every private conversation, the end of every thought and every action, the sole interest of the present.

"It is true," Tocqueville added, "that as soon as the choice is determined, this ardor is dispelled, calm returns, and the river, which had nearly broken its banks, sinks to its usual level; but who can refrain from astonishment that such a storm should have arisen?"

The election storm in the end blows fresh and clean. With the tragic exception of 1860, the American people have invariably accepted the result and given the victor their hopes and blessings. For all its flaws and follies, democracy abides.

Let us now turn the pages and watch the gaudy parade of American presidential politics pass by in all its careless glory.

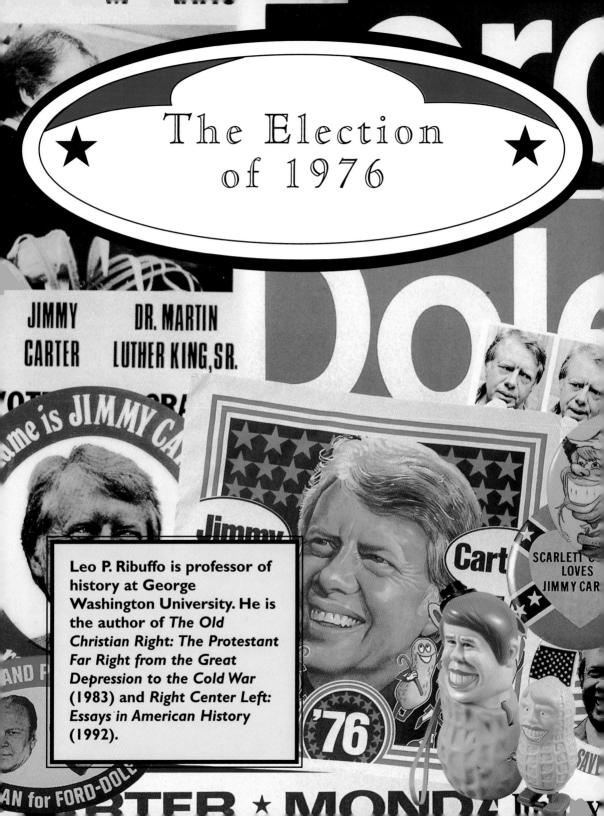

The Election of 1976

Leo P. Ribuffo is professor of history at George Washington University. He is the author of *The Old Christian Right: The Protestant Far Right from the Great Depression to the Cold War* (1983) and *Right Center Left: Essays in American History* (1992).

The presidential election of 1976 was neither the first nor the last in which candidates, commentators, and voters expended great energy on trivial issues, but it was probably the first in which both major party nominees were widely regarded as figures of fun. President Gerald R. Ford was regularly asked whether he was smart enough to be President, and his falls on stairways and ski slopes, frequently satirized on network television, were taken as evidence that he was not. Democratic nominee Jimmy Carter, a "born again" Baptist who tried to explain his faith in *Playboy*, had to contend with what even his own chief adviser, Hamilton Jordan, called the "weirdo factor."

Curiously, neither Ford nor Carter was known for glad-handing, back-slapping, or wit, and the significant questions they addressed with comparable earnestness were unusually serious for a country enjoying relative prosperity and peace. The persistence of both inflation and unemployment—"stagflation"—suggested to some voters that underlying structural weaknesses afflicted the economy. Others, stung by the defeat in Vietnam, worried that the United States was losing the Cold War. The Watergate scandal fostered an amorphous sense that Americans were not so moral as they had thought, and Gerald Ford served as a flesh-and-blood reminder of their discomfort. Appointed by Richard Nixon to replace Vice President Spiro Agnew, who had resigned in disgrace. Ford succeeded Nixon in August 1974 and then, amid rumors of a deal, pardoned Nixon for all crimes related to Watergate.

Not only had the President come to office in unprecedented fashion, but the structure and style of national politics had changed significantly in recent years. Since the election of John F. Kennedy in 1960, presidential aspirants had tried to exude vigor and wit no matter how alien these traits were to their personalities. Questions of personal

Richard Nixon and Spiro Agnew were overwhelmingly re-elected in 1972. However, on October 10, 1973, less then nine months into his second term, Vice President Agnew resigned his office after being charged with extorting bribes from contractors, first while a Maryland county official and then as governor, in exchange for influencing the awarding of government contracts. And, on August 8, 1974, with his presidency engulfed in scandal and his credibility questioned, President Nixon resigned. This is the first time in American history that both a president and vice president did not complete their elected term.

morality were now public issues, and candidates were expected to take positions on abortion as well as arms control. The social upheaval of the late 1960s had strengthened the conservative wing of the Republican Party and shattered the Democratic coalition of hawks and doves, blacks and whites, ardent feminists and cultural traditionalists. The elections of 1964, 1968, and 1972 showed that party outsiders could drive incumbent Presidents from office and even capture the nomination. Federal funding of presidential campaigns, available for the first time in 1976, made such challenges easier to mount.

To an unusual degree, the races for the Republican and Democratic nominations influenced the general election. Ford suffered endless humil-

In 1968, California Governor Ronald Reagan lost the Republican presidential nomination to Richard Nixon. After Nixon was elected, it was widely anticipated that Reagan would seek the presidency at the end of a second Nixon term in 1976. Instead the Watergate affair forced Nixon from office in 1974. Reagan, who had given Nixon the benefit of every doubt during the Watergate inquiry, quickly turned against President Gerald R. Ford and opposed him for the Republican nomination in 1976.

THE
COMPLETE
FORD DOLE
CAMPAIGN MATERIALS
CATALOG
'76

Ford and Dole campaign items. Ford's vice presidential choice of Senator Robert Dole was motivated by the need to heal ideological divisions within the Republican Party.

iation on his road to a narrow victory over the former governor of California, Ronald Reagan. He had trouble finding a competent campaign manager, failed to recognize his party's drift rightward, and underestimated Reagan's political skill. Meanwhile, Reagan assailed Ford as a bumbling product of the Washington "buddy system," whose domestic policies strangled initiative and enriched "welfare queens." In foreign affairs, Ford's pursuit of *détente*, his approval of the Helsinki accords, and his renegotiation of the Panama Canal treaty proved that he lacked the "vision" to reverse the military and diplomatic decline, Reagan postulated. In addition to costing Ford time and money, Reagan's challenge influenced his selection of a combative conservative running mate, Senator Robert Dole of Kansas.

Unlike Ford, Carter felt buoyed by his pre-convention efforts. A one-term governor of Georgia, he had defeated powerful Washington insiders

The peanut became the Carter campaign symbol. Carter's 1975 autobiography, *Why Not the Best?*, gave an idyllic portrait of his youth and his religious and political life.

by combining symbolic politics with careful planning and personal perseverance. Carter understood better than his rivals that the 1976 election was a referendum on American virtue. He would be elected, Carter had said in 1975, if he could "personify in my personal life the aspirations of the American people." His personality was, in fact, many-sided and he shrewdly emphasized different sides of himself to rival Democratic factions. Thus, he was variously a peanut farmer who studied nuclear engineering, an evangelical Protestant who read Reinhold Niebuhr, a white southerner who rejected racism, and a compassionate governor who still wanted balanced budgets. Above all, he was a self-conscious outsider who pledged to lead a government "as good as the people"—people who remained, in Carter's reassuring rhetoric, essentially virtuous despite Vietnam and Watergate.

Hamilton Jordan, pollster Patrick Caddell, and adman Gerald Rafshoon worked to "fine tune" campaign strategy (as Caddell liked to say.) Carter attracted early attention by leading in the Iowa caucuses, won the New Hampshire primary with the help of a volunteer "Peanut Brigade" from Georgia, and courted influential politicians while building grassroots support. Rejecting the labels "conservative" and "liberal," he nonetheless ran to the right of all contenders except George Wallace. Nor did his campaign ignore the post-JFK politics of glamour. Carter adopted a fluffier hairstyle and advertised unlikely "friendships" with rock singers.

All of Carter's symbolism, planning, and perseverance would have counted for little if liberal Democrats had not been divided between avid cold warriors and their dovish critics. Eager for victory, however, all factions rallied around Carter at the national convention in July. Vice presidential nominee Walter Mondale balanced the ticket as a staunch welfare state liberal. Representative Peter Rodino, an ethnic hero of the Watergate scandal, nominated Carter, and Rev. Martin Luther King, Sr., suggested in the benediction that God Himself had ordained Carter to save America.

Despite this celebration, Carter's support was wider than it was deep. Northern working-class Catholics remained wary of his economic conservatism and evangelical demeanor. During the primaries, moreover, Carter's deliberate ambiguities and unintended slips-of-the-tongue had raised doubts about his integrity. According to one joke, Carter could never be honored on Mount Rushmore because there wasn't room for his two faces. Now, for the first time, he encountered in President Ford an opponent capable of exploiting these latent weaknesses.

(Above) Button that links Carter symbolically with Jesus Christ (JC). (Right) Carter pamphlet showing him with Martin Luther King Sr. Black voter turnout had a significant impact on the election.

He's making us proud again.

Poster for Ford. Republican campaign slogans stressed that Ford had restored dignity to the presidency.

Even after winning the nomination in August, Ford trailed Carter by more than twenty points in most polls. After several false starts, however, he put together a superb campaign team from White House Chief of Staff Richard Cheney to public relations specialists at Deardourff and Bailey. According to their analysis, Carter's strategy of displaying various sides of himself to different constituencies could be turned to Ford's advantage by painting the Democratic nominee as a devious opportunist. Conversely, voters liked the President's honesty but, prompted by Carter and Reagan, they questioned his intelligence. Accordingly, while stressing his restoration of good government and preservation of peace, Ford also needed to exude competence and underscore his opponent's inexperience. Blue-collar Catholics were especially susceptible to such appeals if Ford could overcome the issue of high unemployment.

The two nominees circled for position until late September. In his acceptance speech to the Republican convention, which he delivered with atypical fluency, Ford accused Carter of waffling on every major issue and challenged him to debate their differences. Thereafter, he retreated to the White House Rose Garden, hoping to distract attention from the deteriorating economy and the administration's misguided (and often satirized) effort to immunize all Americans against swine flu. Although Carter's strategy was formulated in Atlanta, safely distant from Washington insiders, the candidate's rhetoric was now fine-tuned to attract liberal Democrats. He kicked off his campaign at Franklin D. Roosevelt's little White House in Warm Springs, Georgia, compared himself to Harry S. Truman, and associated Ford with Herbert Hoover as well as Richard Nixon. Meanwhile, Republican and Democratic emissaries struggling to arrange the debates agreed on little beyond the exclusion of independent candidates Lester Maddox and Eugene McCarthy.

In late September the "weirdo factor" flamboyantly surfaced in *Playboy*. Although Carter had granted the magazine an interview partly to demonstrate his own sophistication, his performance left the opposite impression. Warning against self-righteousness, Carter admitted having "looked on many women with lust" and

On September 20, 1976, Robert Scheer's interview with Jimmy Carter for *Playboy* was released to newspapers. While Carter outlined his views on a variety of subjects, what attracted attention was his statement that he often looked at women with "lust in his heart."

"committed adultery in my heart." While supporters vainly pointed to the soundness of his theology, Carter's diverse detractors saw evidence of sand or political naivete. Reporters adapted "Heart Of My Heart" to serenade him.

> Lust in my heart, how I love adultery;
> Lust in my heart, that's my theology.

Prudently sidestepping the lust imbroglio, both candidates reiterated their favorite themes during their first television debate on September 23.

Carter indicted Ford for "lack of leadership" (a failing illustrated by persistent inflation and unemployment approaching 8 percent); promised "comprehensive" programs to restore government efficiency, balance the budget, and reform the tax system; and pledged always to draw "his strength from the people." Ford claimed credit for "turning the economy around" despite fiscally irresponsible congressional Democrats, denigrated Carter's gubernatorial record, and declared that true leaders never try to "be all things to all people." Neither candidate so much as smiled at the other during a twenty-seven minute interruption caused by a technological glitch. Ford sounded knowledgeable and looked dignified in a three-piece suit; benefiting from low expectations, he was judged the winner by most television viewers.

Buoyed by polls showing him within ten points of Carter, Ford escalated his attack. Even the name of his Illinois campaign train, the "Honest Abe," highlighted the integrity he ostentatiously advertised. Fearing that stridency might backfire, Caddell persuaded Carter temporarily to mute personal attacks on Ford and stress the flaws of the "Nixon-Ford administration."

The candidates' families also brought substantive and symbolic messages to the electorate. Betty Ford, an outspoken feminist, had been a liability during the race against Reagan; now she became an asset in appealing to moderate Democrats, some of whom wore buttons declaring, "Keep Betty Ford's Husband in the White House." Carter's forthright and unpretentious wife, Rosalynn, helped him too; she hardly

Transistor radio and wind-up toy satirizing Carter.

seemed the kind of woman who would marry a weirdo. Carter's mother, "Miz Lillian," (who combined humanitarianism with humor) and his brother Billy (who combined a beer belly with blue-collar irreverence) not only softened his prim image but also became celebrities in their own right.

The Republican resurgence faltered on September 30 when Ford learned that a vulgar joke about "coloreds" by Secretary of Agriculture Earl Butz was about to be reported in the media. Carter, impatient with rhetorical fine-tuning, compared this racist remark to an earlier bit of Butz humor about the pope and birth control. Equally troubling to Ford, a special prosecutor had begun to investigate his congressional finances. Thus, while Carter looked forward to resuming the attack, the President prepared less thoroughly for their next debate on October 6.

Carter attacked from both the left and the right. On the one hand, the Nixon-Ford administration betrayed American principles by conducting secret diplomacy, subverting foreign governments, and ignoring international human rights; on the other hand, the Republicans yielded to Arab economic pressure, weakened

Ribbon for Ford issued during the bicentennial celebration.

Group of Ford items. The Ford campaign spent $3 million for fifty state campaign organizations, less than what Nixon had spent in California and New York in 1972.

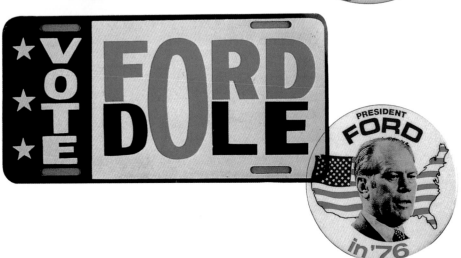

American defenses, and failed to stand "tough" against the Soviet Union. Though generally holding his own, Ford did himself irreparable harm by answering a question that wasn't asked instead of the question that was. Expecting renewed criticism of the Helsinki accords, the President had prepared to say that he did not *concede* the legitimacy of the Soviet sphere in Eastern Europe. Instead, responding to a question about Soviet expansionism, Ford said that there was *in fact* "no Soviet domination of Eastern Europe."

The issue was more complicated than it seemed because countries in Eastern Europe did enjoy varying degrees of autonomy, and American presidents since Truman had tried to maximize that freedom. Carter understood the situation, but such nuances lost their customary appeal in mid-debate. He challenged Ford to persuade Polish-, Czech-, and Hungarian-Americans that "those countries don't live under the domination and supervision of the Soviet Union." Most pundits and reporters did not know the nuances existed. Rather, they presented Ford's debate answer, stubborn refusal to recant, and inarticulate attempts to explain his policy as the latest examples of his chronic befuddlement. The acute phase of the crisis lasted until October 12, when Ford "bluntly" admitted making a "mistake." More important, the question of Ford's competence had been dramatically reopened, and a new round of jokes circulated until election day. After hearing Ford's debate answer, the Washington press corps chuckled, Polish Communist leader Edward Gierek had exclaimed, "Free at last, free at last!"

Discussion of Eastern Europe was one of several low points in the debate between the vice-presidential candidates on October 15. Senator Dole not only accused Democratic presidents of surrendering Eastern Europe to communism, but also attributed 1.6 million casualties to "Democratic wars" in this century. Senator Mondale responded that Dole had "earned his reputation as a hatchet man." Most television viewers agreed.

While the presidential nominees toured the country and held a third, lackluster debate in October, their favorite themes reached the electorate through print, radio, and (especially) television advertisements. In all media, the Republicans played variations on their slogan: "President Ford: He's Making Us Proud Again." A jauntier version of the message, "Feelin' good about America," graced posters, T-shirts, and a song. A biographical TV spot brought Ford from Eagle Scout to the White House and concluded,

"Without seeking the presidency, Gerald Ford has been preparing for it all his life."

Democratic advertisements asked what there was to feel good about. The nation needed "Leadership for a Change" and Carter was the man to provide it. A biographical spot traced his rise from a farm boy in Plains, Georgia (where ads showed him in jeans still working the soil), to national leader. Since half the electorate still considered Dole unqualified for the presidency (according to Caddell's polls), the Democrats often highlighted Mondale as Carter's partner in statesmanship.

Family members played both offense and defense. Miz Lillian reminisced about Carter's youthful hard work; after the *Playboy* fiasco, Rosalynn Carter told viewers that there has never been "any hint of scandal" surrounding her husband. Ford's son Mike, a divinity student, underscored the family's faith in God. At the end of the "Ford family" spot, one of the most effective on either side, the President gently kissed Betty on the cheek.

Advertising professionals adapted or supplemented the general messages for specialized audiences. Echoing a famous newspaper headline that appeared after Ford had rejected federal aid to New York, posters assured subway riders that Carter would "never tell the greatest city on earth to drop dead." In Carter's home region, ads slighted the liberal Mondale in favor of local pride, predicting that "on November 2, the South is being readmitted to the Union." Listeners to radio stations with predominately black audiences learned that Carter's daughter, Amy, attended an integrated school. The Republicans customized their television ads for Hispanics of Cuban, Mexican, and Puerto Rican background, but none could match Carter speaking Spanish in his own spot.

By late October both media campaigns had mastered the techniques of denigration. In Ford's television spots, solid citizens in sequence called Carter "wishy-washy" and Georgians criticized his governorship.

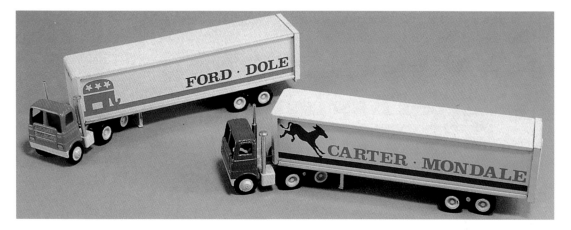

Toy tractor-trailers for Ford and Carter. During the 1976 campaign, Carter had vowed to make the conservation of energy a top priority, calling it "the moral equivalent of war." But his energy program was less ambitious than such rhetoric suggested; interest groups lobbied against various provisions and Congress dismantled much of it. The United States did reduce its oil imports, but Americans paid higher prices for gasoline, and the decisions of the oil-producing nations remained the critical factor in determining those prices.

Exploiting a favorable cover story, a Ford newspaper ad advised: "One good way to decide this election. Read last week's *Newsweek*. Read this month's *Playboy*." The Democrats quoted Ronald Reagan's description of *détente* as a "one-way street." They also tested but ultimately rejected a TV spot explicitly criticizing Ford's pardon of Nixon, apparently realizing that repeated references to the "Nixon-Ford administration" served their purposes without overkill.

The election of 1976 was neither the first nor the last in which adversarial rhetoric obscured basic similarities between the major party nominees, but in this case the discrepancy between purported and actual differences was greater than usual. Both Ford and Carter were devout Protestants from solid middle-class backgrounds. Adapting to the changing political culture, both candidates made subtle religious appeals but both felt uncomfortable doing so. Although Carter rejected and Ford

Celluloid button for Carter evoking the Watergate scandal.

hedged on a proposed Right-to-Life Amendment, both personally opposed abortion and wanted the issue to disappear from presidential politics. Both valued integrity in government, and their occasional lapses into demagoguery were comparably inept. A moderate Republican, Ford was less hostile to the welfare state than he sounded; a fiscally conservative Democrat, Carter was less enthusiastic about the welfare state than he sounded. Though Carter held a deeper visceral commitment to international human rights, he agreed with Ford that containment of the Soviet Union was the central foreign policy concern.

The last week of the campaign was marked by vigorous personal appeals and massive television advertising highlighting the candidates' purported differences. In addition, an incident at the Plains Baptist Church where Carter taught his now famous Sunday school class threatened to undermine liberal and African-American support. Apparently seeking to embarrass Carter, a black minister tried unsuccessfully to attend services and then applied for membership. When the church reaffirmed its old ban on "Negroes and other civil rights agitators," Carter disagreed but declined to resign from the congregation. In telegrams to black clergy, the Republicans asked how Carter could advance the cause of civil rights nationally if he could not influence his own church.

By election eve Ford and Carter stood virtually even in the polls. Ford's last television appeal was primarily a pastiche of earlier ads plus conversations with such non-political friends as baseball announcer Joe Garagiola (who had played everyman in talk shows accompanying the final campaign tour). These conversations took place on *Air Force One*,

(Right) Poster for Carter using the *New York Daily News* headline of October 30, 1975.

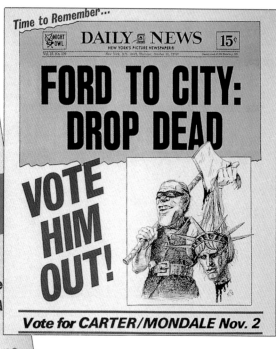

(Left) Poster for Ford using the *New York Daily News* endorsement of Ford, October 23, 1976.

where Ford, hoarse and tired, was almost inaudible. Finally, the plane flew into the sun to the strains of "Feelin' good about America." In his last television appeal, Carter, dressed in a conservative blue suit, answered canned questions from men and women selected to serve as flesh-and-blood symbols of important Democratic constituencies. In a curious turn-about, the Washington insider looked like a worn-out regular guy even though he spoke from the most consequential airplane in the world, and the outsider speaking from Plains, Georgia, looked presidential.

On November 2 Carter led Ford by 1.7 million votes and defeated him in the electoral college 297 to 240. The core of Carter's support came from groups that had voted heavily Democratic since the 1930s, including union members, blacks, and (despite misgivings) northern Catholics; many of

Ford
Dole

(Left) Ford/Dole sticker.
(Right) Enameled metal
pin for Ford.

them were affected by or worried about stagflation. Washington insiders—party professionals and their trade union allies—contributed to the victory by organizing impressive registration and get-out-the-vote drives. Even so, Carter would have lost if he had not attracted lukewarm Democrats and disenchanted Republicans. However weird his religion seemed to cosmopolitan critics, his born-again demeanor attracted Republican evangelicals, and he became the first Democrat since Truman to carry the Southern Baptist vote. Moreover, running against the man who had pardoned Nixon, Carter did manage to personify American aspirations for honesty and virtue in the wake of Vietnam and Watergate.

The narrow defeat prompted Ford and his campaign aides to ponder the might-have-beens. If Ford had taken Reagan seriously from the outset, he might have entered the fall campaign with more money and energy. If Ford had not bogged down in Eastern Europe, he might have preserved the look of competence created in the first debate. If the economic recovery begun earlier in the year had not stalled, Carter's incongruous identification with the New Deal tradition might have been less effective. If

Democratic legal challenges had not removed Eugene McCarthy's name from the ballot in New York, he might have cost Carter that state as he did Oregon and Iowa. If Ford had picked a less conservative—or at least a less abrasive—running mate, he might have carried Ohio or Pennsylvania. Indeed, the election of 1976 was one of few in which the vice presidential nominees made a difference.

In his inaugural address, Jimmy Carter graciously thanked Ford for "all he has done to heal our land." This compliment eased the tension between the two men, who became good friends after Carter left the White House. By that point, their common traits and values were unmistakable, and their common experiences included a disastrous underestimation of Ronald Reagan.

The 1976 election was the first in which the federal government subsidized a campaign. A new law provided for public funds derived from a check-off on the federal income tax form. This law was intended to attract office-seekers who otherwise could not afford to get involved in presidential politics. The Democratic Party also implemented a plan of "affirmative action" to ensure that each state's delegation to their national nominating convention be representative of the population-at-large. Seventy percent of the delegates to the 1976 Democratic Convention were chosen under this new procedure.

However, the most striking feature of the 1976 election was the turnout—the lowest proportion of eligible voters since 1948. Alienated from the political process by the Watergate scandal and distrustful of both candidates, 72 million registered voters made their feelings known on Election Day by staying home.

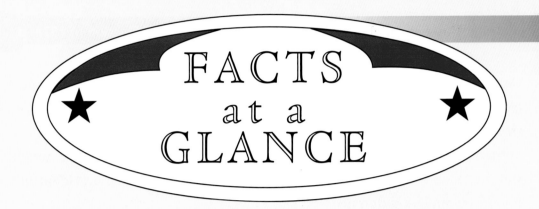

JAMES EARL "JIMMY" CARTER JR.

- **Born:** October 1, 1924, in Plains, Georgia
- **Parents:** James Earl and Lillian Gordy Carter
- **Education:** Graduated from U.S. Naval Academy, Annapolis, MD, in 1946
- **Occupation:** farmer, engineer, public official
- **Married:** Eleanor Rosalynn Smith (1928–   ) on July 7, 1946
- **Children:** John William "Jack" Carter (1947–   ); James Earl "Chip" Carter III (1950–   ); Donnel Jeffrey "Jeff" Carter (1952–   ); Amy Lynn Carter (1967–   )

Served as the 39TH PRESIDENT OF THE UNITED STATES,

- January 20, 1977, to January 20, 1981

VICE PRESIDENT

- Walter F. Mondale (1977–1981)

OTHER POLITICAL POSITIONS

- Georgia State Senator, 1963–66
- Governor of Georgia, 1971–75

CABINET

Secretary of State
- Cyrus R. Vance (1977–80)
- Edmund S. Muskie (1980–81)

Secretary of the Treasury
- W. Michael Blumenthal (1977–79)
- G. William Miller (1979–81)

Secretary of Defense
- Harold Brown (1977–81)

Attorney General
- Griffin B. Bell (1977–79)
- Benjamin R. Civiletti (1979–81)

Secretary of the Interior
- Cecil D. Andrus (1977–81)

Secretary of Agriculture
- Robert S. Bergland (1977–81)

Secretary of Commerce
- Juanita M. Kreps (1977–79)
- Philip Klutznick (1979–81)

Secretary of Labor
- F. Ray Marshall (1977–81)

Secretary of Health, Education, and Welfare
- Joseph A. Califano, Jr. (1977–79)
- Patricia R. Harris (1979–80)

Secretary of Health and Human Services
- Patricia R. Harris (1980–81)

Secretary of Education
- Shirley Hufstedler (1980–81)

Secretary of Housing and Urban Development
- Patricia R. Harris (1977–79)
- Moon Landrieu (1979–81)

Secretary of Transportation
- Brock Adams (1977–79)
- Neil E. Goldschmidt (1979–81)

Secretary of Energy
- James R. Schlesinger (1977–79)
- Charles W. Duncan, Jr. (1979–81)

NOTABLE EVENTS DURING CARTER'S ADMINISTRATION

1977   Inaugurated president on January 20; Congress establishes the departments of education and energy in September; Carter signs the Panama Canal Treaty on September 21; signs International Covenant on Human Rights on November 19.

1978   The Camp David Summit begins on September 4; Camp David Accords signed September 17; in December, Carter announces normalization of relations with People's Republic of China.

1979   Nuclear accident occurs March 28 at Three Mile Island power plant in Pennsylvania; Carter and Soviet premier Leonid Brezhnev sign SALT II treaty in Vienna on June 18; gives "Crisis of Confidence" speech (also called the "malaise speech") on July 15; on November 4, the American Embassy in Tehran, Iran, is attacked by militants at the urging of the religious leader Ayatollah Khomeini and more than 50 Americans are taken hostage; On December 27, the Soviet Union invades Afghanistan.

1980   In January Carter announces sanctions against the Soviet Union to protest their invasion of Afghanistan; in April, a mission to rescue the hostages in Iran fails; Carter loses the presidential election to Republican Ronald Reagan.

1981   Reagan becomes president January 20; Carter goes to Germany to meet the hostages, who were freed moments after Reagan was inaugurated.

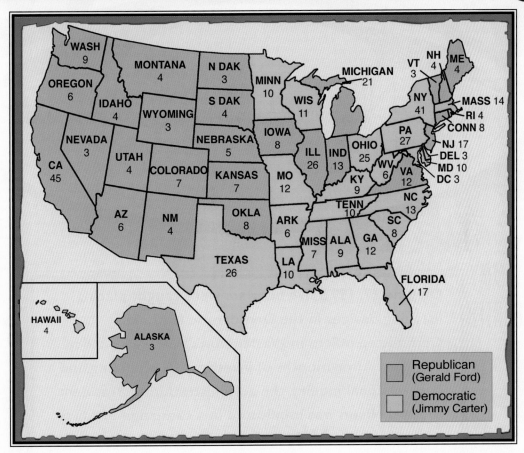

Republican (Gerald Ford)	
Democratic (Jimmy Carter)	

In August 1976, Jimmy Carter had a huge lead in the polls over incumbent Gerald Ford. By November, the gap had narrowed. Carter won 50.1 percent of the popular vote to 48 percent for Ford. Carter received 297 electoral votes, to Ford's 240; Ronald Reagan, who had challenged Ford in the Republican primary, received one of Washington's electoral votes.

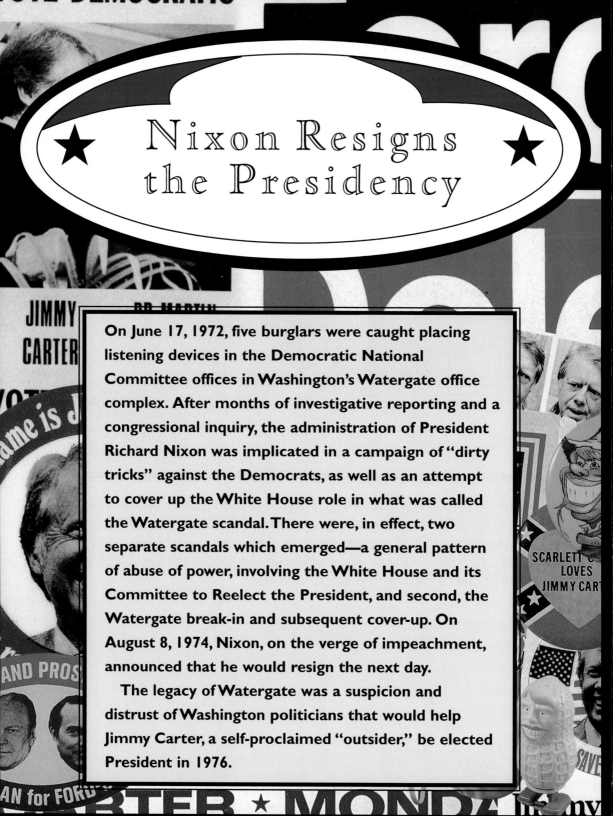

Nixon Resigns the Presidency

On June 17, 1972, five burglars were caught placing listening devices in the Democratic National Committee offices in Washington's Watergate office complex. After months of investigative reporting and a congressional inquiry, the administration of President Richard Nixon was implicated in a campaign of "dirty tricks" against the Democrats, as well as an attempt to cover up the White House role in what was called the Watergate scandal. There were, in effect, two separate scandals which emerged—a general pattern of abuse of power, involving the White House and its Committee to Reelect the President, and second, the Watergate break-in and subsequent cover-up. On August 8, 1974, Nixon, on the verge of impeachment, announced that he would resign the next day.

The legacy of Watergate was a suspicion and distrust of Washington politicians that would help Jimmy Carter, a self-proclaimed "outsider," be elected President in 1976.

Good evening.

This is the 37th time I have spoken to you from this office, where so many decisions have been made that shaped the history of this Nation. Each time I have done so to discuss with you some matter than I believe affected the national interest.

In all the decisions I have made in my public life, I have always tried to do what was best for the Nation. Throughout the long and difficult period of Watergate, I have felt it was my duty to persevere, to make every possible effort to complete the term of office to which you elected me.

In the past few days, however, it has become evident to me that I no longer have a strong enough political base in the Congress to justify continuing that effort. As long as there was such a base, I felt strongly that it was necessary to see the constitutional process through to its conclusion, that to do otherwise would be unfaithful to the spirit of that deliberately difficult process and a dangerously destabilizing precedent for the future.

But with the disappearance of that base, I now believe that the constitutional purpose has been served, and there is no longer a need for the process to be prolonged.

I would have preferred to carry through to the finish whatever the personal agony it would have involved, and my family unanimously urged me to do so. But the interest of the Nation must always come before any personal considerations.

From the discussions I have had with Congressional and other leaders, I have concluded that because of the Watergate matter I might not have the support of the Congress that I would consider necessary to back the very difficult decisions and carry out the duties of this office in the way the interests of the Nation would require.

I have never been a quitter. To leave office before my term is completed is abhorrent to every instinct in my body. But as President, I must put the interest of America first. America needs a full-time President and a full-time Congress, particularly at this time with problems we face at home and abroad.

To continue to fight through the months ahead for my personal vindication would almost totally absorb the time and attention of both the President and the Congress in a period when our entire focus should be on the great issues of peace abroad and prosperity without inflation at home.

Therefore, I shall resign the Presidency effective at noon tomorrow. Vice President Ford will be sworn in as President at that hour in this office.

As I recall the high hopes for America with which we began this second term, I feel a great sadness that I will not be here in this office working on your behalf to achieve those hopes in the next 2 1/2 years. But in turning over direction of the Government to Vice President Ford, I know, as I told the Nation when I nominated him for that office 10 months ago, that the leadership of America will be in good hands.

In passing this office to the Vice President, I also do so with the profound sense of the weight of responsibility that will fall on his shoulders tomorrow and, therefore, of the understanding, the patience, the cooperation he will need from all Americans.

As he assumes that responsibility, he will deserve the help and the support of all of us. As we look to the future, the first essential is to begin healing the wounds of this Nation, to put the bitterness and divisions of the recent past behind us, and to rediscover those shared ideals that lie at the heart of our strength and unity as a great and as a free people.

By taking this action, I hope that I will have hastened the start of that process of healing which is so desperately needed in America.

I regret deeply any injuries that may have been done in the course of the events that led to this decision. I would say only that if some of my judgments were wrong, and some were wrong, they were made in what I believed at the time to be the best interest of the Nation.

To those who have stood with me during these past difficult months, to my family, my friends, to many others who joined in supporting my cause because they believed it was right, I will be eternally grateful for your support.

And to those who have not felt able to give me your support, let me say I leave with no bitterness toward those who have opposed me, because all of us, in the final analysis, have been concerned with the good of the country, however our judgments might differ.

So, let us all now join together in affirming that common commitment and in helping our new President succeed for the benefit of all Americans.

I shall leave this office with regret at not completing my term, but with gratitude for the privilege of serving as your President for the past 5 1/2 years. These years have been a momentous time in the history of our Nation and the world. They have been a time of achievement in which we can all be proud, achievements that represent the shared efforts of the Administration, the Congress, and the people.

But the challenges ahead are equally great, and they, too, will require the support and the efforts of the Congress and the people working in cooperation with the new Administration.

We have ended America's longest war, but in the work of securing a lasting peace in the world, the goals ahead are even more far-reaching and more difficult. We must complete a structure of peace so that it will be said of this generation, our generation of Americans, by the people of all nations, not only that we ended one war but that we prevented future wars.

We have unlocked the doors that for a quarter of a century stood between the United States and the People's Republic of China.

We must now ensure that the one quarter of the world's people who live in the People's Republic of China will be and remain not our enemies but our friends.

In the Middle East, 100 million people in the Arab countries, many of whom have considered us their enemy for nearly 20 years, now look on us as their friends. We must continue to build on that friendship so that peace can settle at last over the Middle East and so that the cradle of civilization will not become its grave.

Together with the Soviet Union we have made the crucial breakthroughs that have begun the process of limiting nuclear arms. But we must set as our goal not just limiting but reducing and finally destroying these terrible weapons so that they cannot destroy civilization and so that the threat of nuclear war will no longer hang over the world and the people.

We have opened the new relation with the Soviet Union. We must continue to develop and expand that new relationship so that the two strongest nations of the world will live together in cooperation rather than confrontation.

Around the world, in Asia, in Africa, in Latin America, in the Middle East, there are millions of people who live in terrible poverty, even starvation. We must keep as our goal turning away from production for war and expanding production for peace so that people everywhere on this earth can at last look forward in their children's time, if not in our own time, to having the necessities for a decent life.

Here in America, we are fortunate that most of our people have not only the blessings of liberty but also the means to live full and good and, by the world's standards, even abundant lives. We must press on, however, toward a goal of not only more and better jobs but of full opportunity for every American and of what we are striving so hard right now to achieve, prosperity without inflation.

For more than a quarter of a century in public life I have shared in the turbulent history of this era. I have fought for what I believed in. I have tried to the best of my ability to discharge those duties and meet those responsibilities that were entrusted to me.

Sometimes I have succeeded and sometimes I have failed, but always I have taken heart from what Theodore Roosevelt once said about the man in the arena, "whose face is marred by dust and sweat and blood, who strives valiantly, who errs and comes short again and again because there is not effort without error and shortcoming, but who does actually strive to do the deed, who knows the great enthusiasms, the great devotions, who spends himself in a worthy cause, who at the best knows in the end the triumphs of high achievements and who at the worst, if he fails, at least fails while daring greatly."

I pledge to you tonight that as long as I have a breath of life in my body, I shall continue in that spirit. I shall continue to work for the great causes to which I have been dedicated throughout my years as a Congressman, a Senator, a Vice President, and President, the cause of peace not just for America but among all nations, prosperity, justice, and opportunity for all of our people.

There is one cause above all to which I have been devoted and to which I shall always be devoted for as long as I live.

When I first took the oath of office as President 5 1/2 years ago, I made this sacred commitment, to "consecrate my office, my energies, and all the wisdom I can summon to the cause of peace among nations."

I have done my very best in all the days since to be true to that pledge. As a result of these efforts, I am confident that the world is a safer place today, not only for the people of America but for the people of all nations, and that all of our children have a better chance than before of living in peace rather than dying in war.

This, more than anything, is what I hoped to achieve when I sought the Presidency. This, more than anything, is what I hope will be my legacy to you, to our country, as I leave the Presidency.

To have served in this office is to have felt a very personal sense of kinship with each and every American. In leaving it, I do so with this prayer: May God's grace be with you in all the days ahead.

★ Ford's Remarks on ★ Becoming President

"Our long national nightmare is over," proclaimed Gerald R. Ford on August 9, 1974, as he took the oath of office as the 38th president of the United States. The new president was personable, hardworking, and honest. To most Americans, these were attractive qualities after their recent political experience.

On no issue—domestic or foreign—were there any discernible differences between Ford and Nixon. Since 1949, when Ford was elected to the House of Representatives, he had reflected the views of his conservative Michigan constituency. As House minority leader, he had won the respect of Democrats and Republicans because of his candor and even temper.

Ford is the first person in American history to be appointed to fill a vacancy in the vice presidency and the only vice president to become president upon the resignation of the president—and the first president to reach the White House through the procedure established by the Twenty-fifth Amendment (1967).

The oath that I have taken is the same oath that was taken by George Washington and by every President under the Constitution. But I assume the Presidency under extraordinary circumstances never before experienced by Americans. This is an hour of history that troubles our minds and hurts our hearts.

Therefore, I feel it is my first duty to make an unprecedented compact with my countrymen. Not an inaugural address, not a fireside chat, not a campaign speech—just a little straight talk among friends. And I intend it to be the first of many.

I am acutely aware that you have not elected me as your President by your ballots, and so I ask you to confirm me as your President with your prayers. And I hope that such prayers will also be the first of many.

If you have not chosen me by secret ballot, neither have I gained office by any secret promises. I have not campaigned either for the Presidency or the Vice Presidency. I have not subscribed to any partisan platform. I am indebted to no man, and only to one woman—my dear wife—as I begin this very difficult job.

I have not sought this enormous responsibility, but I will not shirk it. Those who nominated and confirmed me as Vice President were my friends and are my friends. They were of both parties, elected by all the people and acting under the Constitution in their name. It is only fitting then that I should pledge to them and to you that I will be the President of all the people.

Thomas Jefferson said the people are the only sure reliance for the preservation of our liberty. And down the years, Abraham Lincoln renewed this American article of faith asking, "Is there any better way or equal hope in the world?"

I intend, on Monday next, to request of the Speaker of the House of Representatives and the President pro tempore of the Senate the privilege of appearing before the Congress to share with my former colleagues and with you, the American people, my views on the priority business of the Nation and to solicit your views and their views. And may I say to the Speaker and the others, if I could meet with you right after these remarks, I would appreciate it.

Even though this is late in an election year, there is no way we can go forward except together and no way anybody can win except by serving the people's urgent needs. We cannot stand still or slip backwards. We must go forward now together.

To the peoples and the governments of all friendly nations, and I hope that could encompass the whole world, I pledge an uninterrupted and sincere search for peace. America will remain strong and united, but its strength will remain dedicated to the safety and sanity of the entire family of man, as well as to our own precious freedom.

I believe that truth is the glue that holds government together, not only our

Less than two years after he won reelection by as huge a margin as any in American history, Nixon resigned from office in defeat and humiliation.

Government but civilization itself. That bond, though strained, is unbroken at home and abroad.

In all my public and private acts as your President, I expect to follow my instincts of openness and candor with full confidence that honesty is always the best policy in the end.

My fellow Americans, our long national nightmare is over.

Our Constitution works; our great Republic is a government of laws and not of men. Here the people rule. But there is a higher Power, by whatever name we honor Him, who ordains not only righteousness but love, not only justice but mercy.

As we bind up the internal wounds of Watergate, more painful and more poisonous than those of foreign wars, let us restore the golden rule to our political process, and let brotherly love purge our hearts of suspicion and of hate.

In the beginning, I asked you to pray for me. Before closing, I ask again your prayers, for Richard Nixon and for his family. May our former President, who brought peace to millions, find it for himself. May God bless and comfort his wonderful wife and daughters, whose love and loyalty will forever be a shining legacy to all who bear the lonely burdens of the White House.

I can only guess at those burdens, although I have witnessed at close hand the tragedies that befell three Presidents and the lesser trials of others.

With all the strength and all the good sense I have gained from life, with all the confidence my family, my friends, and my dedicated staff impart to me, and with the good will of countless Americans I have encountered in recent visits to 40 States, I now solemnly reaffirm my promise I made to you last December 6—to uphold the Constitution, to do what is right as God gives me to see the right, and to do the very best I can for America.

God helping me, I will not let you down.

Thank you.

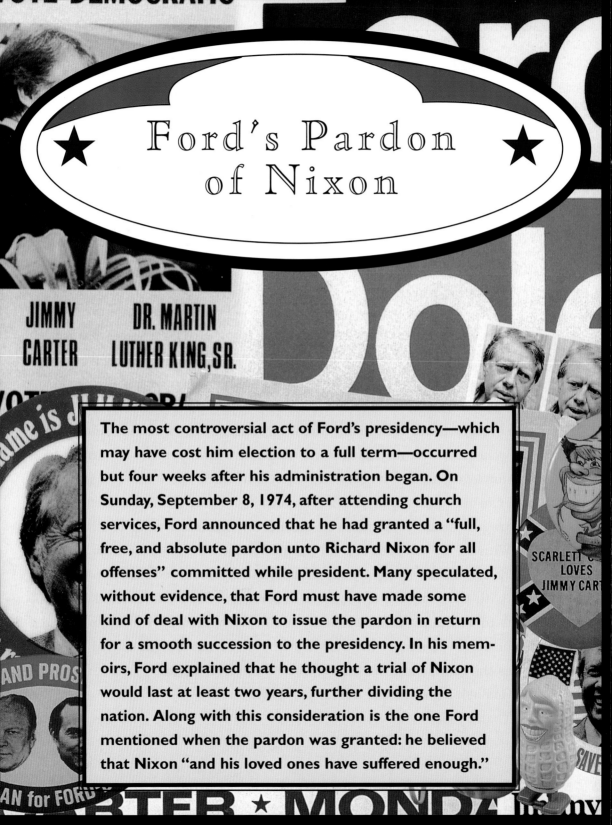

Ford's Pardon of Nixon

The most controversial act of Ford's presidency—which may have cost him election to a full term—occurred but four weeks after his administration began. On Sunday, September 8, 1974, after attending church services, Ford announced that he had granted a "full, free, and absolute pardon unto Richard Nixon for all offenses" committed while president. Many speculated, without evidence, that Ford must have made some kind of deal with Nixon to issue the pardon in return for a smooth succession to the presidency. In his memoirs, Ford explained that he thought a trial of Nixon would last at least two years, further dividing the nation. Along with this consideration is the one Ford mentioned when the pardon was granted: he believed that Nixon "and his loved ones have suffered enough."

By the President of the United States of America a Proclamation:

Richard Nixon became the thirty-seventh President of the United States on January 20, 1969, and was reelected in 1972 for a second term by the electors of forty-nine of the fifty states. His term in office continued until his resignation on August 9, 1974.

Pursuant to resolutions of the House of Representatives, its Committee on the Judiciary conducted an inquiry and investigation on the impeachment of the President extending over more than eight months. The hearings of the Committee and its deliberations, which received wide national publicity over television, radio, and in printed media, resulted in votes adverse to Richard Nixon on recommended Articles of Impeachment.

As a result of certain acts or omissions occurring before his resignation from the Office of President, Richard Nixon has become liable to possible indictment and trial for offenses against the United States. Whether or not he shall be so prosecuted depends on findings of the appropriate grand jury and on the discretion of the authorized prosecutor. Should an indictment ensue, the accused shall then be entitled to a fair trial by an impartial jury, as guaranteed to every individual by the Constitution.

It is believed that a trial of Richard Nixon, if it became necessary, could not fairly begin until a year or more has elapsed. In the meantime, the tranquility to which this nation has been restored by the events of recent weeks could be irreparably lost by the prospects of bringing to trial a former President of the United States. The prospects of such trial will cause prolonged and divisive debate over the propriety of exposing to further punishment and degradation a man who has already paid the unprecedented penalty of relinquishing the highest elective office of the United States.

After the exhausting Watergate ordeal, the good feelings of the first weeks of President Ford's administration came as a relief. Ford's selection of Governor Nelson Rockefeller of New York as vice president pleased Republican moderates.

Ford was faced with the immediate task of naming his own vice president and thus establishing the first unelected term of a president and vice president in American history. He nominated Nelson A. Rockefeller, recently retired after four terms as governor of New York. Rockefeller, who unsuccessfully had sought the Republican presidential nomination three times, was the leader of the party's moderate faction. Rockefeller's selection was designed to give Ford a vice president with expertise and experience in domestic policy planning and implementation. However, protracted congressional nomination hearings delayed Rockefeller's confirmation for four months. In 1976, conservative opposition to Rockefeller forced Ford to choose a different running mate for the Republican ticket. Ford admitted in his memoirs: "I was angry with myself in not saying to the ultraconservatives, 'It's going to be Ford and Rockefeller, whatever the consequences.'"

Now, Therefore, I, Gerald R. Ford, President of the United States, pursuant to the pardon power conferred upon me by Article II, Section 2, of the Constitution, have granted and by these presents do grant a full, free, and absolute pardon unto Richard Nixon for all offenses against the United States which he, Richard Nixon, has committed or may have committed or taken part in during the period from January 20, 1969, through August 9, 1974.

In Witness Whereof, I have hereunto set my hand this eighth day of September, in the year of our Lord nineteen hundred and seventy-four, and of the Independence of the United States of America the one hundred and ninety-ninth.

Poster for Ford and Dole. Memories of Vietnam, Watergate, and the Nixon pardon haunted Ford throughout the campaign of 1976. His strategy was to be "presidential."

Ford Accepts the Nomination

Ford expected little difficulty in obtaining the 1976 Republican nomination. However, he was startled by Ronald Reagan's insurgent candidacy. The former California governor was extremely popular among party conservatives. In fact, Ford's policies throughout 1976 were deeply affected by his eagerness to appease the Republican right. On August 18, 1976, Ford won the nomination on the first ballot—1,187 to 1,070. Reagan did so well because party rules gave western and southwestern states a disproportionate share of the delegates. (A July 1976 Gallup Poll showed the president leading among Republicans by 61 to 31 percent.) "You at home, listening tonight, you are the people who pay taxes and obey the laws," Ford said in his acceptance speech. "It is from your ranks that I come and on your side I stand." At the end of the speech, he invited Reagan to the podium to address the delegates.

I am honored by your nomination, and I accept it with pride, with gratitude, and with a total will to win a great victory for the American people. We will wage a winning campaign in every region of this country, from the snowy banks of Minnesota to the sandy plains of Georgia. We concede not a single State. We concede not a single vote.

This evening I am proud to stand before this great convention as the first incumbent President since Dwight D. Eisenhower who can tell the American people America is at peace.

Tonight I can tell you straightaway this Nation is sound, this Nation is secure, this Nation is on the march to full economic recovery and a better quality of life for all Americans.

And I will tell you one more thing: This year the issues are on our side. I am ready, I am eager to go before the American people and debate the real issues face to face with Jimmy Carter.

The American people have a right to know firsthand exactly where both of us stand.

I am deeply grateful to those who stood with me in winning the nomination of the party whose cause I have served all of my adult life. I respect the convictions of those who want a change in Washington. I want a change, too. After 22 long years of majority misrule, let's change the United States Congress.

My gratitude tonight reaches far beyond this arena to countless friends whose confidence, hard work, and unselfish support have brought me to this moment. It would be unfair to single out anyone, but may I make an exception for my wonderful family—Mike, Jack, Steve, and Susan and especially my dear wife, Betty.

We Republicans have had some tough competition. We not only preach the virtues of competition, we practice them. But tonight we come together not on a battlefield to conclude a cease-fire, but to join forces on a training field that has conditioned us all for the rugged contest ahead. Let me say this from the bottom of my heart: After the scrimmages of the past few months, it really feels good to have Ron Reagan on the same side of the line.

To strengthen our championship lineup, the convention has wisely chosen one of the ablest Americans as our next Vice President, Senator Bob Dole of Kansas. With his help, with your help, with the help of millions of Americans who cherish peace, who want freedom preserved, prosperity shared, and pride in America, we will win this election. I speak not of a Republican victory, but a victory for the American people.

You at home listening tonight, you are the people who pay the taxes and obey the laws. You are the people who make our system work. You are the people who make America what it is. It is from your ranks that I come and on your side that I stand.

Something wonderful happened to this country of ours the past two years. We all came to realize it on the Fourth of July. Together, out of years of turmoil and tragedy, wars and riots, assassinations and wrongdoing in high places, Americans recaptured the spirit of 1776. We saw again the pioneer vision of our revolutionary founders and our immigrant ancestors. Their vision was of free men and free women enjoying limited government and unlimited opportunity. The mandate I want in 1976 is to make this vision a reality, but it will take the voices and the votes of many more Americans who are not Republicans to make that mandate binding and my mission possible.

I have been called an unelected President, an accidental President. We may even hear that again from the other party, despite the fact that I was welcomed and endorsed by an overwhelming majority of their elected representatives in the Congress who certified my fitness to our highest office. Having become Vice President and President without expecting or seeking either, I have a special feeling toward these high offices. To me, the Presidency and the Vice-Presidency were not prizes to be won, but a duty to be done.

So, tonight it is not the power and the glamour of the Presidency that leads

Ford campaign items. Ford and Carter had three televised debates, the first between presidential candidates since the Kennedy-Nixon exchanges in 1960. Although television was replacing traditional campaign materials, 1976 did see a variety of posters, buttons, and novelty items.

me to ask for another four years; it is something every hard-working American will understand-the challenge of a job well begun, but far from finished.

Two years ago, on August 9, 1974, 1 placed my hand on the Bible, which Betty held, and took the same constitutional oath that was administered to George Washington. I had faith in our people, in our institutions, and in myself. "My fellow Americans," I said, "our long national nightmare is over."

It was an hour in our history that troubled our minds and tore at our hearts. Anger and hatred had risen to dangerous levels, dividing friends and families. The polarization of our political order had aroused unworthy passions of reprisal and revenge. Our governmental system was closer to stalemate than at any time since Abraham Lincoln took the same oath of office. Our economy was in the throes of runaway inflation, taking us headlong into the worst recession since Franklin D. Roosevelt took the same oath. [. . .]

On a marble fireplace in the White House is carved a prayer which John Adams wrote. It concludes, "May none but honest and wise men ever rule under this roof." Since I have resided in that historic house, I have tried to live by that prayer. I faced many tough problems. I probably made some mistakes, but on balance, America and Americans have made an incredible comeback since August 1974. Nobody can honestly say otherwise. And the plain truth is that the great progress we have made at home and abroad was in spite of the majority who run the Congress of the United States.

For two years I have stood for all the people against a vote-hungry, free-spending congressional majority on Capitol Hill. Fifty-five times I vetoed extravagant and unwise legislation; 45 times I made those vetoes stick. Those vetoes have saved American taxpayers billions and billions of dollars. I am against the big tax spender and for the little taxpayer.

I called for a permanent tax cut, coupled with spending reductions, to stimulate the economy and relieve hard-pressed, middle-income taxpayers. Your personal exemption must be raised from $750 to $1,000. The other party's platform talks about tax reform, but there is one big problem—their own Congress won't act.

I called for reasonable constitutional restrictions on court-ordered busing of schoolchildren, but the other party's platform concedes that busing should be a last resort. But there is the same problem—their own Congress won't act.

I called for a major overhaul of criminal laws to crack down on crime and illegal drugs. The other party's platform deplores America's $90 billion cost of crime. There is the problem again—their own Congress won't act.

The other party's platform talks about a strong defense. Now, here is the other side of the problem—their own Congress did act. They slashed $50 billion from our national defense needs in the last 10 years.

My friends, Washington is not the problem; their Congress is the problem.

You know, the President of the United States is not a magician who can wave a wand or sign a paper that will instantly end a war, cure a recession, or make bureaucracy disappear. A President has immense powers under the Constitution, but all of them ultimately come from the American people and their mandate to him. That is why, tonight, I turn to the American people and ask not only for your prayers but also for your strength and your support, for your voice, and for your vote.

I come before you with a two-year record of performance without your mandate. I offer you a four-year pledge of greater performance with your mandate. As Governor Al Smith used to say, "Let's look at the record."

Two years ago inflation was 12 percent. Sales were off. Plants were shut down. Thousands were being laid off every week.

Fear of the future was throttling down our economy and threatening millions of families.

Let's look at the record since August 1974. Inflation has been cut in half. Payrolls are up. Profits are up. Production is up. Purchases are up. Since the recession was turned around, almost 4 million of our fellow Americans have found new jobs or got their old jobs back. This year more men and women have jobs than ever before in the history of the United States. Confidence has returned, and we are in the full surge of sound recovery to steady prosperity.

Two years ago America was mired in withdrawal from Southeast Asia. A decade of Congresses had shortchanged our global defenses and threatened our strategic posture. Mounting tension between Israel and the Arab nations made another war seem inevitable. The whole world watched and wondered where America was going. Did we in our domestic turmoil have the will, the stamina, and the unity to stand up for freedom?

Look at the record since August, two years ago. Today America is at peace and seeks peace for all nations. Not a single American is at war anywhere on the face of this Earth tonight.

Our ties with Western Europe and Japan, economic as well as military, were never stronger. Our relations with Eastern Europe, the Soviet Union, and mainland China are firm, vigilant, and forward looking. Policies I have initiat-

ed offer sound progress for the peoples of the Pacific, Africa, and Latin America. Israel and Egypt, both trusting the United States, have taken an historic step that promises an eventual just settlement for the whole Middle East.

The world now respects America's policy of peace through strength. The United States is again the confident leader of the free world. Nobody questions our dedication to peace, but nobody doubts our willingness to use our strength when our vital interests are at stake, and we will. I called for an up-to-date, powerful Army, Navy, Air Force, and Marines that will keep America secure for decades. A strong military posture is always the best insurance for peace. But America's strength has never rested on arms alone. It is rooted in our mutual commitment of our citizens and leaders in the highest standards of ethics and morality and in the spiritual renewal which our Nation is undergoing right now.

Two years ago people's confidence in their highest officials, to whom they had overwhelmingly entrusted power, had twice been shattered. Losing faith in the word of their elected leaders, Americans lost some of their own faith in themselves.

Again, let's look at the record since August 1974. From the start my administration has been open, candid, forthright. While my entire public and private life was under searching examination for the Vice-Presidency, I reaffirmed my lifelong conviction that truth is the glue that holds government together—not only government but civilization itself. I have demanded honesty, decency, and personal integrity from everybody in the executive branch of the Government. The House and Senate have the same duty.

The American people will not accept a double standard in the United States Congress. Those who make our laws today must not debase the reputation of our great legislative bodies that have given us such giants as Daniel Webster, Henry Clay, Sam Rayburn, and Robert A. Taft. Whether in the nation's capital, the state capital, or city hall, private morality and public trust must go together.

From August of 1974 to August of 1976, the record shows steady progress upward toward prosperity, peace, and public trust. My record is one of progress, not platitudes. My record is one of specifics, not smiles. My record is one of performance, not promises. It is a record I am proud to run on. It is a record the American people—Democrats, Independents, and Republicans alike—will support on November 2.

For the next four years I pledge to you that I will hold to the steady course we have begun. But I have no intention of standing on the record alone.

We will continue winning the fight against inflation. We will go on reducing the dead weight and impudence of bureaucracy.

We will submit a balanced budget by 1978.

We will improve the quality of life at work, at play, and in our homes and in our neighborhoods. We will not abandon our cities. We will encourage urban programs which assure safety in the streets, create healthy environments, and restore neighborhood pride. We will return control of our children's education to parents and local school authorities.

We will make sure the party of Lincoln remains the party of equal rights.

We will create a tax structure that is fair for all citizens, one that preserves the continuity of the family home, the family farm, and the family business.

We will ensure the integrity of [social security] and improve Medicare so that our older citizens can enjoy the health and the happiness that they have earned. There is no reason they should have to go broke just to get well.

We will make sure that this rich Nation does not neglect citizens who are less fortunate, but provides for their needs with compassion and with dignity.

We will reduce the growth and the cost of government and allow individual breadwinners and businesses to keep more of the money that they earn.

We will create a climate in which our economy will provide a meaningful job for everyone who wants to work and a decent standard of life for all Americans. We will ensure that all of our young people have a better chance in life than we had, an education they can use, and a career they can be proud of.

We will carry out a farm policy that assures a fair market price for the farmer, encourages full production, leads to record exports, and eases the hunger within the human family. We will never use the bounty of America's farmers as a pawn in international diplomacy. There will be no embargoes.

We will continue our strong leadership to bring peace, justice, and economic progress where there is turmoil, especially in the Middle East. We will build a safer and saner world through patient negotiations and dependable arms agreements which reduce the danger of conflict and horror of thermonuclear war. While I am President, we will not return to a collision course that could reduce civilization to ashes.

We will build an America where people feel rich in spirit as well as in worldly goods. We will build an America where people feel proud about themselves and about their country.

We will build on performance, not promises; experience, not expediency; real progress instead of mysterious plans to be revealed in some dim and distant future. The American people are wise, wiser than our opponents think. They know who pays for every campaign promise. They are not afraid of the truth. We will tell them the truth.

From start to finish, our campaign will be credible; it will be responsible. We will come out fighting, and we will win. Yes, we have all seen the polls and the pundits who say our party is dead. I have heard that before. So did Harry Truman. I will tell you what I think. The only polls that count are the polls the American people go to on November 2. And right now, I predict that the American people are going to say that night, "Jerry, you have done a good job, keep right on doing it."

As I try in my imagination to look into the homes where families are watching the end of this great convention, I can't tell which faces are Republicans, which are Democrats, and which are Independents. I cannot see their color or their creed. I see only Americans.

I see Americans who love their husbands, their wives, and their children. I see Americans who love their country for what it has been and what it must become. I see Americans who work hard, but who are willing to sacrifice all they have worked for to keep their children and their country free. I see Americans who in their own quiet way pray for peace among nations and peace among themselves. We do love our neighbors, and we do forgive those who have trespassed against us.

I see a new generation that knows what is right and knows itself, a generation determined to preserve its ideals, its environment, our Nation, and the world.

My fellow Americans, I like what I see. I have no fear for the future of this great country. And as we go forward together, I promise you once more what I promised before: to uphold the Constitution, to do what is right as God gives me to see the right, and to do the very best that I can for America.

God helping me, I won't let you down.

Thank you very much.

Carter Accepts the Nomination

JIMMY CARTER   DR. MARTIN LUTHER KING, SR.

In January 1976, a Gallup Poll of Democrats reported that only 4 percent favored Carter as their party's candidate. The following week, Carter won the caucuses in Iowa with 27.6 percent of those who designated a candidate. "None of the above" received just less than 30 percent. Nevertheless, *Time* proclaimed him the Democratic front runner. In the "make or break" Pennsylvania preferential vote, Carter received 37 percent of the vote. A *Washington Post* exit poll showed that 46 percent of the voters would have favored Hubert Humphrey had he been a candidate. Nevertheless, the "Anyone but Carter" effort by labor leaders and political professionals failed. Carter won the nomination of the first ballot at the Democratic Convention. He chose Senator Walter Mondale of Minnesota as his running mate.

My name is Jimmy Carter, and I'm running for president. It's been a long time since I said those words the first time, and now I've come here, after seeing our great country, to accept your nomination.

I accept it in the words of John F. Kennedy: "With a full and grateful heart—and with only one obligation—to devote every effort of body, mind and spirit to lead our party back to victory and our nation back to greatness."

It's a pleasure to be with all you Democrats and to see that our Bicentennial celebration and our Bicentennial convention has been one of decorum and order, without any fights or free-for-alls. Among Democrats, that could only happen once every 200 years.

With this kind of a united Democratic Party, we are ready and eager to take on the Republicans, whichever Republican Party they decide to send against us in November.

1976 will not be a year of politics as usual. It can be a year of inspiration and hope. And it will be a year of concern, of quiet and sober reassessment of our nation's character and purpose—a year when voters have already confounded the experts.

And I guarantee you that it will be the year when we give the government of this country back to the people of this country.

There's a new mood in America.

We have been shaken by a tragic war abroad and by scandals and broken promises at home. Our people are searching for new voices and new ideas and new leaders.

Although government has its limits and cannot solve all our problems, we Americans reject the view that we must be reconciled to failures and mediocrity, or to an inferior quality of life.

For I believe that we can come through this time of trouble stronger than ever. Like troops who've been in combat, we've been tempered in the fire—we've been disciplined and we've been educated. Guided by lasting and simple moral values, we've emerged idealists without illusions, realists who still know the old dreams of justice and liberty—of country and community. [. . .]

We've been a nation adrift too long. We've been without leadership too long. We've had divided and deadlocked government too long. We've been governed by veto too long. We've suffered enough at the hands of a tired and worn-out administration without new ideas, without youth or vitality, without visions, and without the confidence of the American people.

There is a fear that our best years are behind us, but I say to you that our nation's best is still ahead. [. . .]

It's time for the people to run the government, and not the other way around. It's time to honor and strengthen our families and our neighborhoods, and our diverse cultures and customs.

We need a Democratic president and a Congress to work in harmony for a change, with mutual respect for a change, in the open for a change, and next year we are going to have that new leadership. You can depend on it.

It's time for America to move and speak, not with boasting and belligerence, but with a quiet strength—to depend in world affairs not merely on the size of an arsenal but on the nobility of ideas—and to govern at home not by confusion and crisis but with grace and imagination and common sense.

Too many have had to suffer at the hands of a political and economic elite who have shaped decisions and never had to account for mistakes nor to suffer from injustice. When unemployment prevails, they never stand in line looking for a job. When deprivation results from a confused and bewildering welfare system, they never do without food or clothing or a place to sleep. When the public schools are inferior or torn by strife, their children go to exclusive private schools. And when the bureaucracy is bloated and confused, the powerful always manage to discover and occupy niches of special influence and privilege. An unfair tax structure serves their needs. And tight secrecy always seems to prevent reform. [. . .]

Jimmy Carter, former governor of Georgia, won the Democratic nomination because he had a superb grasp of the complex rules of the new primary system. He sensed the mood of the nation's disillusionment which was caused by the Vietnam war and the Watergate scandal. The fact that the public had little perception of what Carter was really like enabled him to shape an image to meet the demands of the new political reality.

Carter built his organization in key states with little money and only a few aides. He decided to base his campaign in his hometown of Plains, Georgia, allowing reporters to see for themselves the virtues of a friendly, small, rural, southern town. As he campaigned for the nomination across the country, Carter emphasized his personal character. He pledged that he would never lie to the American people, and that he was committed to "open government." His autobiography *Why Not the Best?* gave an idyllic portrait of his roots and a confirmation and description of his deep Christian faith.

Carter proclaimed himself as a new kind of political leader, one who could heal the nation's wounds. But he was deliberately vague on issues. As he stated on *Face the Nation* in March 1976, the voters "just feel that I'm the sort of person they can trust, and if they are liberal, I think I'm compatible with their views. If they are moderate, the same; and if the voter is conservative, I think they'll still feel that I'm a good President." It seemed inconceivable that the Democrats would choose someone who held no current office, had no strong power base, and who came from the Deep South.

Too often, unholy, self-perpetuating alliances have been formed between money and politics, and the average citizen has been held at arm's length.

Each time our nation has made a serious mistake, the American people have been excluded from the process. The tragedy of Vietnam and Cambodia, the disgrace of Watergate, and the embarrassment of the CIA revelations could have been avoided if our government had simply reflected the sound judgement and good common sense and the high moral character of the American people.

It's time for us to take a new look at our own government, to strip away the secrecy, to expose the unwarranted pressure of lobbyists, to eliminate waste, to release our civil servants from bureaucratic chaos, to provide tough management and always to remember that in any town or city, the mayor, the governor and the president represent exactly the same constituents.

As a governor, I had to deal each day with the complicated and confused and overlapping and wasteful federal government bureaucracy. As president, I want you to help me evolve an efficient, economical, purposeful and manageable government for our nation. Now I recognize the difficulty, but if I'm elected, it's going to be done, and you can depend on it.

We must strengthen the government closest to the people.

Business, labor, agriculture, education, science education, government should not struggle in isolation from one another, but should be able to strive toward mutual goals and shared opportunities.

We should make major investments in people and not in buildings and weapons. The poor, the aged, the weak, the afflicted must be treated with respect and compassion and with love.

Now I have spoken a lot of times this year about love, but love must be aggressively translated into simple justice.

The test of any government is not how popular it is with the powerful, but how honestly and fairly it deals with those who must depend on it.

It's time for a complete overhaul of our income tax system. I still tell you it's a disgrace to the human race. All my life I have heard promises of tax reform, but it never quite happens. With your help, we are finally going to make it happen and you can depend on it.

Here is something that can really help our country.

It's time for universal voter registration.

It's time for a nationwide, comprehensive health program for all our people.

It's time to guarantee an end to discrimination because of race or sex by full involvement in the decision-making processes of government by those who

Carter button from the 1976 campaign. While campaigning for the Democratic presidential nomination, Carter began most of his speeches with the announcement, "My name is Jimmy Carter, and I'm running for president." He repeated this mantra as he accepted the party's nomination in July 1976.

know what it is to suffer from discrimination, and they'll be in the government if I'm elected.

It's time for the law to be enforced. We cannot educate children, we cannot create harmony among our people, we cannot preserve basic human freedom unless we have an orderly society. Now crime and a lack of justice are especially cruel to those who are least able to protect themselves. Swift arrest and trial, and fair and uniform punishment should be expected by anyone who would break our laws.

It's time for our government leaders to respect the law no less than the humblest citizen, so that we can end once and for all a double standard of justice. I see no reason why big shot crooks should go free and the poor ones go to jail.

A simple and a proper function of government is just to make it easy for us to do good and difficult for us to do wrong.

Now as an engineer, a planner, and a businessman, I see clearly the value to our nation of a strong system of free enterprise based an increased productivity and adequate wages. We Democrats believe that competition is better than regulation. And we intend to combine strong safeguards for consumers with minimal intrusion of government in our free economic system.

I believe that anyone who is able to work ought to work—and ought to have a chance to work. We'll never end the inflationary spiral, we'll never have a balanced budget, which I am determined to see, as long as we have eight or nine million Americans out of work who cannot find a job.

Now any system of economics is bankrupt if it sees either value or virtue in unemployment. We simply cannot check inflation by keeping people out of work.

The foremost responsibility of any President above all else is to guarantee the security of our nation—a guarantee of freedom from the threat of successful attack or blackmail and the ability with our allies to maintain peace.

But peace is not the mere absence of war. Peace is action to stamp out international terrorism. Peace is the unceasing effort to preserve human rights. And peace is a combined demonstration of strength and good will. We'll pray for peace and we'll work for peace, until we have removed from all nations for all time the threat of nuclear destruction.

America's birth opened a new chapter in mankind's history. Ours was the first nation to dedicate itself clearly to basic moral and philosophical principles—that all people are created equal and endowed with inalienable rights to life, liberty and the pursuit of happiness; and that the power of government is derived from the consent of the governed.

This national commitment was a singular act of wisdom and courage, and

Republican button poking fun at one of Carter's campaign symbols, the peanut. During the campaign Carter was portrayed as a simple peanut farmer from Georgia who would "clean up" Washington.

it brought the best and the bravest from other nations to our shores.

It was a revolutionary development that captured the imagination of mankind.

It created the basis for a unique role for America—that of a pioneer shaping more decent and just relations among people and among societies.

Today, 200 years later, we must address ourselves to that role both in what we do at home and how we act abroad—among people everywhere who have become politically more alert, socially more congested and increasingly impatient with global inequities, and who are now organized as you know, into some 50 different nations.

This calls for nothing less than a sustained architectural effort to shape an international framework of peace within which our own ideals gradually can become a global reality.

Our nation should always derive its character directly from the people and let this be the strength and the image to be presented to the world—the character of the American people.

To our friends and allies I say that what unites us through our common dedication to democracy is much more important than that in which occasionally divides us on economics or politics.

To the nations that seek to lift themselves from poverty, I say that America shares your aspirations and extends its hand to you.

To those nation-states that wish to compete with us, I say that we neither fear competition nor see it as an obstacle to wider cooperation.

And to all people I say that after 200 years America still remains confident and youthful in its commitment to freedom and equality, and we always will be.

During this election year, we candidates will ask you for your votes, and from us will be demanded our vision.

My vision of this nation and its future has been deepened and matured during the 19 months that I have campaigned among you for President.

I've never had more faith in America than I do today.

We have an America that, in Bob Dylan's phrase, is busy being born, not busy dying.

We can have an American government that's turned away from scandal and corruption and official cynicism and is once again as decent and competent as our people.

We can have an America that has reconciled its economic needs with its desire for an environment we can pass on with pride to the next generation.

We can have an America that provides excellence in education to my child and your child and every child. We can have an America that encourages and takes pride in our ethnic diversity, our religious diversity, our cultural diversity knowing that out of this pluralistic heritage has come the strength and the vitality and the creativity that made us great and will keep us great.

We can have an American government that does not oppress or spy on its own people, but respects our dignity and our privacy and our right to be let alone.

We can have an America where freedom on the one hand and equality on the other hand are mutually supportive and not in conflict, and where the dreams of our nation's first leaders are fully realized in our own day and age.

And we can have an America which harnesses the idealism of the student, the compassion of the nurse or the social worker, the determination of the farmer, the wisdom of a teacher, the practicality of the business leader, the experience of the senior citizen and the hope of a laborer to build a better life for us all, and we can have it and we are gonna have it.

As I've said many times before, we can have an American president who does not govern with negativism and fear of the future, but with vigor and vision and aggressive leadership—a President who's not isolated from the people, but who feels your pain and shares your dreams, and takes his strength and his wisdom and his courage from you.

I see an America on the move again, united, a diverse and vital and tolerant nation, entering our third century with pride and confidence—an America that lives up to the majesty of our Constitution and the simple decency of our people.

This is the America we want.

This is the America that we will have.

We'll go forward from this convention with some differences of opinion, perhaps, but nevertheless united in a calm determination to make our country large and driving and generous in spirit once again, ready to embark on great national deeds. And once again, as brothers and sisters, our hearts will swell with pride to call ourselves Americans.

Thank you very much.

Perhaps unhappiness with the economy, and a general disenchantment with Ford, enabled Carter to win a narrow victory— 50 percent of the popular vote to Ford's 47.9 percent and 297 electoral votes to Ford's 240. This was the closest victory since Woodrow Wilson's 1916 win over Charles Evans Hughes.

In describing his inauguration, Carter wrote in his diary: "Even though I had been preparing to be President, I was genuinely surprised when in the benediction, the Bishop from Minnesota referred to 'blessings on President Carter.' Just the phrase 'President Carter,' was startling to me." For the swearing-in ceremony, Carter used his campaign name, "Jimmy Carter," rather than the formal James Earl Carter Jr. He took the oath of office on a Bible that had been in the family for four generations. After an unusually brief address, the traditional parade down Pennsylvania Avenue to the White House began. Carter, attempting to emulate Jefferson's efforts to identify with the "common man," broke with tradition by walking the mile and a half with his wife and daughter at his side. Not since Jefferson had a president walked in his inaugural parade.

For myself and for our Nation, I want to thank my predecessor for all he has done to heal our land.

In this outward and physical ceremony we attest once again to the inner and spiritual strength of our Nation. As my high school teacher, Miss Julia Coleman, used to say: "We must adjust to changing times and still hold to unchanging principles."

Here before me is the Bible used in the inauguration of our first President, in 1789, and I have just taken the oath of office on the Bible my mother gave me a few years ago, opened to a timeless admonition from the ancient prophet Micah: "He hath showed thee, O man, what is good; and what doth the Lord require of thee, but to do justly, and to love mercy, and to walk humbly with thy God." [Micah 6:8]

This inauguration ceremony marks a new beginning, a new dedication within our Government, and a new spirit among us all. A President may sense and proclaim that new spirit, but only a people can provide it.

Two centuries ago our Nation's birth was a milestone in the long quest for freedom, but the bold and brilliant dream which excited the founders of this Nation still awaits its consummation. I have no new dream to set forth today, but rather urge a fresh faith in the old dream.

Ours was the first society openly to define itself in terms of both spirituality and of human liberty. It is that unique self-definition which has given us an exceptional appeal, but it also imposes on us a special obligation, to take on those moral duties which, when assumed, seem invariably to be in our own best interests.

You have given me a great responsibility—to stay close to you, to be worthy of you, and to exemplify what you are. Let us create together a new national spirit of unity and trust. Your strength can compensate for my weakness, and your wisdom can help to minimize my mistakes.

Let us learn together and laugh together and work together and pray together, confident that in the end we will triumph together in the right.

The American dream endures. We must once again have full faith in our country and in one another. I believe America can be better. We can be even stronger than before.

Let our recent mistakes bring a resurgent commitment to the basic principles of our Nation, for we know that if we despise our own government we have no future. We recall in special times when we have stood briefly, but magnificently, united. In those times no prize was beyond our grasp.

But we cannot dwell upon remembered glory. We cannot afford to drift. We reject the prospect of failure or mediocrity or an inferior quality of life for any person. Our Government must at the same time be both competent and compassionate.

We have already found a high degree of personal liberty, and we are now struggling to enhance equality of opportunity. Our commitment to human rights must be absolute, our laws fair, our natural beauty preserved; the powerful must not persecute the weak, and human dignity must be enhanced.

We have learned that "more" is not necessarily "better," that even our great Nation has its recognized limits, and that we can neither answer all questions nor solve all problems. We cannot afford to do everything, nor can we afford to lack boldness as we meet the future. So, together, in a spirit of individual sacrifice for the common good, we must simply do our best.

Our Nation can be strong abroad only if it is strong at home. And we know that the best way to enhance freedom in other lands is to demonstrate here that our democratic system is worthy of emulation.

To be true to ourselves, we must be true to others. We will not behave in foreign places so as to violate our rules and standards here at home, for we know that the trust which our Nation earns is essential to our strength.

The world itself is now dominated by a new spirit. Peoples more numerous and more politically aware are craving and now demanding their place in the sun—not just for the benefit of their own physical condition, but for basic

CHALLENGING LEADERSHIP FOR CHALLENGING TIMES

CARTER ★ MONDALE
FOR PRESIDENT ★ FOR VICE PRESIDENT

human rights.

The passion for freedom is on the rise. Tapping this new spirit, there can be no nobler nor more ambitious task for America to undertake on this day of a new beginning than to help shape a just and peaceful world that is truly humane.

We are a strong nation, and we will maintain strength so sufficient that it need not be proven in combat—a quiet strength based not merely on the size of an arsenal, but on the nobility of ideas.

We will be ever vigilant and never vulnerable, and we will fight our wars against poverty, ignorance, and injustice—for those are the enemies against which our forces can be honorably marshaled.

We are a purely idealistic Nation, but let no one confuse our idealism with weakness.

Because we are free we can never be indifferent to the fate of freedom elsewhere. Our moral sense dictates a clear-cut preference for these societies which share with us an abiding respect for individual human rights. We do not seek to intimidate, but it is clear that a world which others can dominate with impunity would be inhospitable to decency and a threat to the well-being of all people.

The world is still engaged in a massive armaments race designed to ensure continuing equivalent strength among potential adversaries. We pledge perseverance and wisdom in our efforts to limit the world's armaments to those necessary for each nation's own domestic safety. And we will move this year a step toward ultimate goal—the elimination of all nuclear weapons from this Earth. We urge all other people to join us, for success can mean life instead of death.

Within us, the people of the United States, there is evident a serious and purposeful rekindling of confidence. And I join in the hope that when my time as your President has ended, people might say this about our Nation:

- that we had remembered the words of Micah and renewed our search for humility, mercy, and justice;

- that we had torn down the barriers that separated those of different race and region and religion, and where there had been mistrust, built unity, with a respect for diversity;

- that we had found productive work for those able to perform it;

- that we had strengthened the American family, which is the basis of our society;

- that we had ensured respect for the law, and equal treatment under the law, for the weak and the powerful, for the rich and the poor;

- and that we had enabled our people to be proud of their own Government once again.

I would hope that the nations of the world might say that we had built a lasting peace, built not on weapons of war but on international policies which reflect our own most precious values.

These are not just my goals, and they will not be my accomplishments, but the affirmation of our Nation's continuing moral strength and our belief in an undiminished, ever-expanding American dream.

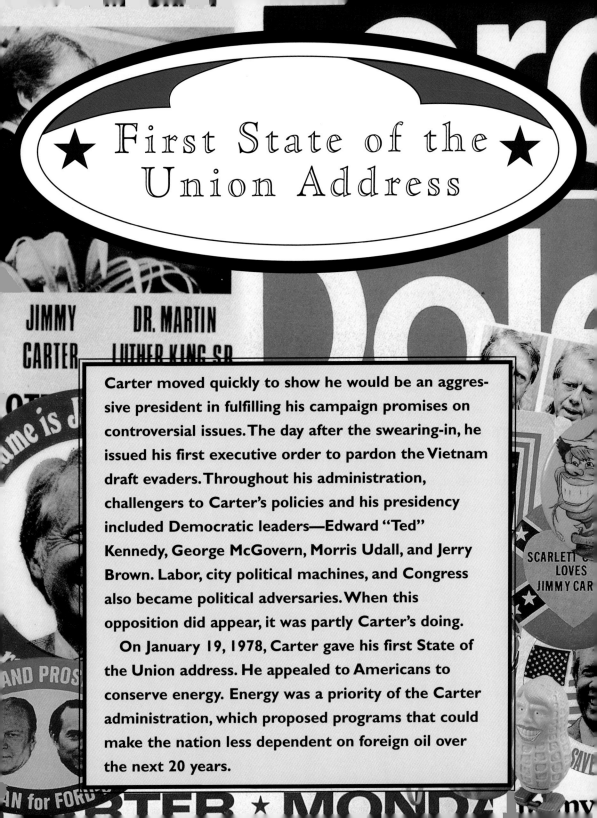

★ First State of the Union Address ★

Carter moved quickly to show he would be an aggressive president in fulfilling his campaign promises on controversial issues. The day after the swearing-in, he issued his first executive order to pardon the Vietnam draft evaders. Throughout his administration, challengers to Carter's policies and his presidency included Democratic leaders—Edward "Ted" Kennedy, George McGovern, Morris Udall, and Jerry Brown. Labor, city political machines, and Congress also became political adversaries. When this opposition did appear, it was partly Carter's doing.

On January 19, 1978, Carter gave his first State of the Union address. He appealed to Americans to conserve energy. Energy was a priority of the Carter administration, which proposed programs that could make the nation less dependent on foreign oil over the next 20 years.

Two years ago today we had the first caucus in Iowa, and one year ago tomorrow, I walked from here to the White House to take up the duties of President of the United States. I didn't know it then when I walked, but I've been trying to save energy ever since.

I return tonight to fulfill one of those duties of the Constitution: to give to the Congress, and to the Nation, information on the state of the Union.

Militarily, politically, economically, and in spirit, the state of our Union is sound.

We are a great country, a strong country, a vital and dynamic country, and so we will remain.

We are a confident people and a hardworking people, a decent and a compassionate people, and so we will remain.

I want to speak to you tonight about where we are and where we must go, about what we have done and what we must do. And I want to pledge to you my best efforts and ask you to pledge yours.

Each generation of Americans has to face circumstances not of its own choosing, but by which its character is measured and its spirit is tested.

There are times of emergency, when a nation and its leaders must bring their energies to bear on a single urgent task. That was the duty Abraham Lincoln faced when our land was torn apart by conflict in the War Between the States. That was the duty faced by Franklin Roosevelt when he led America out of an economic depression and again when he led America to victory in war.

There are other times when there is no single overwhelming crisis, yet profound national interests are at stake.

At such times the risk of inaction can be equally great. It becomes the task of leaders to call forth the vast and restless energies of our people to build for the future.

That is what Harry Truman did in the years after the Second World

War, when we helped Europe and Japan rebuild themselves and secured an international order that has protected freedom from aggression.

We live in such times now, and we face such duties.

We've come through a long period of turmoil and doubt, but we've once again found our moral course, and with a new spirit, we are striving to express our best instincts to the rest of the world.

There is all across our land a growing sense of peace and a sense of common purpose. This sense of unity cannot be expressed in programs or in legislation or in dollars. It's an achievement that belongs to every individual American. This unity ties together, and it towers over all our efforts here in Washington, and it serves as an inspiring beacon for all of us who are elected to serve.

This new atmosphere demands a new spirit, a partnership between those of us who lead and those who elect. The foundations of this partnership are truth, the courage to face hard decisions, concern for one another and the common good over special interests, and a basic faith and trust in the wisdom and strength and judgment of the American people.

For the first time in a generation, we are not haunted by a major international crisis or by domestic turmoil, and we now have a rare and a priceless opportunity to address persistent problems and burdens which come to us as a nation, quietly and steadily getting worse over the years.

As President, I've had to ask you, the Members of Congress, and you, the American people, to come to grips with some of the most difficult and hard questions facing our society.

We must make a maximum effort, because if we do not aim for the best, we are very likely to achieve little. I see no benefit to the country if we delay, because the problems will only get worse.

We need patience and good will, but we really need to realize that there is a limit to the role and the function of government. Government cannot solve our problems, it can't set our goals, it cannot define our vision. Government

Carter-Mondale poster in Spanish.

While it is difficult to point to one factor in such a close election, Carter did extremely well with men, winning a greater share of their vote than any Democrat during the previous 25 years, with the exception of Lyndon Johnson. After voting nearly alike in 1972, men and women diverged in 1976. Ford would have been elected by a 51-48 percent margin in an all-female America.

If credit for putting Carter in the White House can be claimed by any single group, non-whites might justifiably make such a claim. They voted for Carter by more than a five-to-one margin, contributing to Carter's electoral win in New York, Louisiana, Mississippi and Texas. White voters alone would have elected Ford by a comfortable 52-46 percent.

Jimmy Carter/Walter Mondale

To Bring America Together Again

En el Espíritu del '76

Por Empleo Pleno y Plenitud de Vida

International Ladies Garment Workers Union · 1710 Broadway, New York, New York
Sol C. Chaikin, President

cannot eliminate poverty or provide a bountiful economy or reduce inflation or save our cities or cure illiteracy or provide energy. And government cannot mandate goodness. Only a true partnership between government and the people can ever hope to reach these goals.

Those of us who govern can sometimes inspire, and we can identify needs and marshal resources, but we simply cannot be the managers of everything and everybody.

We here in Washington must move away from crisis management, and we must establish clear goals for the future, immediate and the distant future, which will let us work together and not in conflict. Never again should we neglect a growing crisis like the shortage of energy, where further delay will only lead to more harsh and painful solutions.

Every day we spend more than $120 million for foreign oil. This slows our economic growth, it lowers the value of the dollar overseas, and it aggravates unemployment and inflation here at home.

Now we know what we must do, increase production. We must cut down on waste. And we must use more of those fuels which are plentiful and more permanent. We must be fair to people, and we must not disrupt our Nation's economy and our budget.

Now, that sounds simple. But I recognize the difficulties involved. I know that it is not easy for the Congress to act. But the fact remains that on the energy legislation, we have failed the American people. Almost five years after the oil embargo dramatized the problem for us all, we still do not have a national energy program. Not much longer can we tolerate this stalemate. It undermines our national interest both at home and abroad. We must succeed, and I believe we will.

Our main task at home this year, with energy a central element, is the Nation's economy. We must continue the recovery and further cut unemployment and inflation.

Last year was a good one for the United States. We reached all of our major economic goals for 1977. Four million new jobs were created, an all-time record, and the number of unemployed dropped by more than a million. Unemployment right now is the lowest it has been since 1974, and not since World War II has such a high percentage of American people been employed.

The rate of inflation went down. There was a good growth in business profits and investments, the source of more jobs for our workers, and a higher standard of living for all our people. After taxes and inflation, there was a healthy increase in workers' wages.

And this year, our country will have the first $2 trillion economy in the history of the world.

Now, we are proud of this progress the first year, but we must do even better in the future.

We still have serious problems on which all of us must work together. Our trade deficit is too large. Inflation is still too high, and too many Americans still do not have a job.

Now, I didn't have any simple answers for all these problems. But we have developed an economic policy that is working, because it's simple, balanced, and fair. It's based on four principles:

• First, the economy must keep on expanding to produce new jobs and better income, which our people need. The fruits of growth must be widely shared. More jobs must be made available to those who have been bypassed until now. And the tax system must be made fairer and simpler.

• Secondly, private business and not the Government must lead the expansion in the future.

• Third, we must lower the rate of inflation and keep it down. Inflation slows down economic growth, and it's the most cruel to the poor and also to the elderly and others who live on fixed incomes.

• And fourth, we must contribute to the strength of the world economy. [. . .]

In a separate written message to Congress, I've outlined other domestic initiatives, such as welfare reform, consumer protection, basic education skills, urban policy, reform of our labor laws, and national health care later on this year. I will not repeat these tonight. But there are several other points that I would like to make directly to you.

During these past years, Americans have seen our Government grow far from us.

For some citizens, the Government has almost become like a foreign coun-

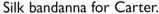

Silk bandanna for Carter.

try, so strange and distant that we've often had to deal with it through trained ambassadors who have sometimes become too powerful and too influential, lawyers, accountants, and lobbyists. This cannot go on.

We must have what Abraham Lincoln wanted, a government for the people.

We've made progress toward that kind of government. You've given me the authority I requested to reorganize the Federal bureaucracy. And I am using that authority.

We've already begun a series of reorganization plans which will be completed over a period of 3 years. We have also proposed abolishing almost 500 Federal advisory and other commissions and boards. But I know that the American people are still sick and tired of Federal paperwork and red tape. Bit by bit we are chopping down the thicket of unnecessary Federal regulations by which Government too often interferes in our personal lives and our personal business. We've cut the public's Federal paperwork load by more than 12 percent in less than a year. And we are not through cutting.

We've made a good start on turning the gobbledygook of Federal regulations into plain English that people can understand. But we know that we still have a long way to go.

We've brought together parts of 11 Government agencies to create a new Department of Energy. And now it's time to take another major step by creating a separate Department of Education.

But even the best organized Government will only be as effective as the people who carry out its policies. For this reason, I consider civil service reform to be absolutely vital. Worked out with the civil servants themselves, this reorganization plan will restore the merit principle to a system which has grown into a bureaucratic maze. It will provide greater management flexibility and better rewards for better performance without compromising job security.

Then and only then can we have a government that is efficient, open, and truly worthy of our people's understanding and respect. I have promised that we will have such a government, and I intend to keep that promise.

We Americans have a great deal of work to do together. In the end, how well we do that work will depend on the spirit in which we approach it. We must seek fresh answers, unhindered by the stale prescriptions of the past.

It has been said that our best years are behind us. But I say again that America's best is still ahead. We have emerged from bitter experiences chastened but proud, confident once again, ready to face challenges once again, and united once again. [. . .]

Our task, to use the words of Senator Humphrey, is "reconciliation, rebuilding, and rebirth."

Reconciliation of private needs and interests into a higher purpose.

Rebuilding the old dreams of justice and liberty, and country and community.

Rebirth of our faith in the common good.

Each of us here tonight, and all who are listening in your homes, must rededicate ourselves to serving the common good. We are a community, a beloved community, all of us. Our individual fates are linked, our futures intertwined. And if we act in that knowledge and in that spirit, together, as the Bible says, we can move mountains.

Thank you very much.

★ Carter Speaks on the Panama Canal ★

Carter came to Washington promising fundamental changes in America's role in world affairs. His agenda emphasized human rights, nuclear disarmament, and a curtailment of American arms sales abroad. None achieved much success, although human rights remains as an ideal and disarmament has followed the end of the Cold War. Ironically, Carter's most notable successes in foreign policy came through conventional diplomacy. The idea of returning the Panama Canal to Panama had begun in the Johnson Administration and continued under Presidents Nixon and Ford. Opponents of returning the Canal, including Ronald Reagan and conservatives from both parties, cited the loss of American honor and the jeopardy to national security. In 1977, the debate dominated the Senate for eight months with impressive speeches on both sides. The debate continued, pro and con, in editorials and talk shows across the country. In April 1978, with one vote to spare, the Senate passed the treaty. Prior to the vote, Carter explained why he thought the Canal should be returned to Panama.

Seventy-five years ago, our Nation signed a treaty which gave us rights to build a canal across Panama, to take the historic step of joining the Atlantic and Pacific Oceans. The results of the agreement have been of great benefit to ourselves and to other nations throughout the world who navigate the high seas.

The building of the canal was one of the greatest engineering feats of history. Although massive in concept and construction, it's relatively simple in design and has been reliable and efficient in operation. We Americans are justly and deeply proud of this great achievement.

The canal has also been a source of pride and benefit to the people of Panama—but a cause of some continuing discontent. Because we have controlled a 10-mile-wide strip of land across the heart of their country and because they considered the original terms of the agreement to be unfair, the people of Panama have been dissatisfied with the treaty. It was drafted here in our country and was not signed by any Panamanian. Our own Secretary of State who did sign the original treaty said it was "vastly advantageous to the United States and . . . not so advantageous to Panama."

In 1964, after consulting with former Presidents Truman and Eisenhower, President Johnson committed our Nation to work towards a new treaty with the Republic of Panama. And last summer, after 14 years of negotiation under two Democratic Presidents and two Republican Presidents, we reached and signed an agreement that is fair and beneficial to both countries. The United States Senate will soon be debating whether these treaties should be ratified.

Throughout the negotiations, we were determined that our national security interests would be protected; that the canal would always be open and neutral and available to ships of all nations; that in time of need or emergency our warships would have the right to go to the head of the line for priority passage through the canal; and that our military forces would have the permanent right to defend the canal if it should ever be in danger. The new treaties meet all of these requirements.

Let me outline the terms of the agreement. There are two treaties—one covering the rest of this century, and the other guaranteeing the safety, openness, and neutrality of the canal after the year 1999, when Panama will be in charge of its operation.

For the rest of this century, we will operate the canal through a nine-person board of directors. Five members will be from the United States and four will be from Panama. Within the area of the present Canal Zone, we have the right to select whatever lands and waters our military and civilian forces need to maintain, to operate, and to defend the canal.

About 75 percent of those who now maintain and operate the canal are Panamanians; over the next 22 years, as we manage the canal together, this percentage will increase. The Americans who work on the canal will continue to have their rights of employment, promotion, and retirement carefully protected.

We will share with Panama some of the fees paid by shippers who use the canal. As in the past, the canal should continue to be self-supporting.

This is not a partisan issue. The treaties are strongly backed by President Gerald Ford and by former secretaries of state Dean Rusk and Henry Kissinger. They are endorsed by our business and professional leaders, especially those who recognize the benefits of good will and trade with other nations in this hemisphere. And they were endorsed overwhelmingly by the Senate Foreign Relations Committee which, this week, moved closer to ratification by approving the treaties, although with some recommended changes which we do not feel are needed.

And the treaties are supported enthusiastically by every member of the Joint Chiefs of Staff—General George Brown, the Chairman, General Bernard Rogers, Chief of Staff of the Army, Admiral James Holloway, Chief of Naval

Operations, General David Jones, Chief of Staff of the Air Force, and General Louis Wilson, Commander of the Marine Corps—responsible men whose profession is the defense of this Nation and the preservation of our security.

The treaties also have been overwhelmingly supported throughout Latin America, but predictably, they are opposed abroad by some who are unfriendly to the United States and who would like to see disorder in Panama and a disruption of our political, economic, and military ties with our friends in Central and South America and in the Caribbean.

I know that the treaties also have been opposed by many Americans. Much of that opposition is based on misunderstanding and misinformation. I've found that when the full terms of the agreement are known, most people are convinced that the national interests of our country will be served best by ratifying the treaties.

Tonight, I want you to hear the facts. I want to answer the most serious questions and tell you why I feel the Panama Canal treaties should be approved.

The most important reason—the only reason—to ratify the treaties is that they are in the highest national interest of the United States and will strengthen our position in the world. Our security interests will be stronger. Our trade opportunities will be improved. We will demonstrate that as a large and powerful country, we are able to deal fairly and honorably with a proud but smaller sovereign nation. We will honor our commitment to those engaged in world commerce that the Panama Canal will be open and available for use by their ships—at a reasonable and competitive cost—both now and in the future.

Let me answer specifically the most common question about the treaties.

Will our Nation have the right to protect and defend the canal against any armed attack or threat to the security of the canal or of ships going through it?

The answer is yes, and is also contained in both treaties and also in the statement of understanding between the leaders of our two nations.

The first treaty says, and I quote: "The United States of America and the Republic of Panama commit themselves to protect and defend the Panama Canal. Each Party shall act, in accordance with its constitutional processes, to meet the danger resulting from an armed attack or any other actions which threaten the security of the Panama Canal or [of] ships transiting it."

The neutrality treaty says, and I quote again: "The United States of America and the Republic of Panama agree to maintain the regime of neutrality established in this Treaty, which shall be maintained in order that the Canal shall remain permanently neutral. . . ."

And to explain exactly what that means, the statement of understanding says, and I quote again: "Under (the Neutrality Treaty), Panama and the United States have the responsibility to assure that the Panama Canal will remain open and secure to ships of all nations. The correct interpretation of this principle is that each of the two countries shall, in accordance with their respective constitutional processes, defend the Canal against any threat to the regime of neutrality, and consequently [shall] have the right to act against the Canal or against the peaceful transit of vessels through the Canal."

It is obvious that we can take whatever military action is necessary to make sure that the canal always remains open and safe.

Of course, this does not give the United States any right to intervene in the internal affairs of Panama, nor would our military action ever be directed against the territorial integrity or the political independence of Panama.

Military experts agree that even with the Panamanian Armed Forces joined with us as brothers against a common enemy, it would take a large number of American troops to ward off a heavy attack. I, as President, would not hesitate to deploy whatever armed forces are necessary to defend the canal, and I have no doubt that even in a sustained combat, that we would be successful. But there is a much better way than sending our sons and grandsons to fight in the jungles of Panama.

We would serve our interests better by implementing the new treaties, an action that will help to avoid any attack on the Panama Canal.

What we want is the permanent right to use the canal—and we can defend this right through the treaties—through real cooperation with Panama. The citizens of Panama and their government have already shown their support of the new partnership, and a protocol to the neutrality treaty will be signed by many other nations, thereby showing their strong approval.

The new treaties will naturally change Panama from a passive and sometimes deeply resentful bystander into an active and interested partner, whose vital interests will be served by a well-operated canal. This agreement leads to cooperation and not confrontation between our country and Panama.

Another question is: Why should we give away the Panama Canal Zone? As many people say, "We bought it, we paid for it, it's ours."

I must repeat a very important point: We do not own the Panama Canal Zone. We have never had sovereignty over it. We have only had the right to use it.

The Canal Zone cannot be compared with United States territory. We bought Alaska from the Russians, and no one has ever doubted that we own it. We bought the Louisiana Purchases—Territories from France, and that's an integral part of the United States.

From the beginning, we have made an annual payment to Panama to use their land. You do not pay rent on your own land. The Panama Canal Zone has always been Panamanian territory. The U.S. Supreme Court and previous American Presidents have repeatedly acknowledged the sovereignty of Panama over the Canal Zone.

We've never needed to own the Panama Canal Zone, any more than we need to own a 10-mile-wide strip of land all the way through Canada from Alaska when we build an international gas pipeline.

The new treaties give us what we do need—not ownership of the canal, but the right to use it and to protect it. As the Chairman of the Joint Chiefs of

Staff has said, "The strategic value of the canal lies in its use."

There's another question: Can our naval ships, our warships, in time of need or emergency, get through the canal immediately instead of waiting in line?

The treaties answer that clearly by guaranteeing that our ships will always have expeditious transit through the canal. To make sure that there could be no possible disagreement about what these words mean, the joint statement says that the expeditious transit, and I quote, "is intended . . . to assure the transit of such vessels through the Canal as quickly as possible, without any impediment, with expedited treatment, and in case of need or emergency, to go to the head of the line of vessels in order to transit the Canal rapidly."

Will the treaties affect our standing in Latin America? Will they create a so-called power vacuum, which our enemies might move in to fill? They will do just the opposite. The treaties will increase our Nation's influence in this hemisphere, will help to reduce any mistrust and disagreement, and they will remove a major source of anti-American feeling.

The new agreement has already provided vivid proof to the people of this hemisphere that a new era of friendship and cooperation is beginning and that what they regard as the last remnant of alleged American colonialism is being removed.

Last fall, I met individually with the leaders of 18 countries in this hemisphere. Between the United States and Latin America there is already a new sense of equality, a new sense of trust and mutual respect that exists because of the Panama Canal treaties. This opens up a fine opportunity for us in good will, trade, jobs, exports, and political cooperation.

If the treaties should be rejected, this would all be lost, and disappointment and despair among our good neighbors and traditional friends would be severe.

In the peaceful struggle against alien ideologies like communism, these treaties are a step in the right direction. Nothing could strengthen our competitors and adversaries in this hemisphere more than for us to reject the agreement.

What if a new sea-level canal should be needed in the future? This question has been studied over and over throughout this century, from before the time the canal was build through the last few years. Every study has reached the same conclusion—that the best place to build a sea-level canal is in Panama.

The treaties say that if we want to build such a canal, we will build it in Panama, and if any canal is to be built in Panama, that we, the United States, will have the right to participate in the project.

This is a clear benefit to us, for it ensures that, say, 10 or 20 years from now, no unfriendly but wealthy power will be able to purchase the right to build a sea-level canal, to bypass the existing canal, perhaps leaving that other nation in control of the only usable waterway across the isthmus.

Are we paying Panama to take the canal? We are not. Under the new treaty, any payments to Panama will come from tolls paid by ships which use the canal.

What about the present and the future stability and the capability of the Panamanian Government? Do the people of Panama themselves support the agreement?

Well, as you know, Panama and her people have been our historical allies and friends. The present leader of Panama has been in office for more than nine years, and he heads a stable government which has encouraged the development of free enterprise in Panama. Democratic elections will be held this August to choose the members of the Panamanian Assembly, who will in turn elect a President and a Vice President by majority vote. In the past, regimes have changed in Panama, but for 75 years, no Panamanian government has ever wanted to close the canal.

Panama wants the canal open and neutral—perhaps even more than we do. The canal's continued operation is very important to us, but it is much more than that to Panama. To Panama, it's crucial. Much of her economy flows directly or indirectly from the canal. Panama would be no more likely to neglect or close the canal than we would be to close the Interstate Highway System here in the United States.

In an open and free referendum last October, which was monitored very carefully by the United Nations, the people of Panama gave the new treaties their support.

The major threat to the canal comes not from any government of Panama, but from misguided persons who may try to fan the flames of dissatisfaction with the terms of the old treaty.

There's a final question—about the deeper meaning of the treaties themselves, to us and to Panama.

Recently, I discussed the treaties with David McCullough, author of *The Path Between the Seas*, the great history of the Panama Canal. He believes that the canal is something that we built and have looked after these many years; it is "ours" in that sense, which is very different from just ownership.

So, when we talk of the canal, whether we are old, young, for or against the treaties, we are talking about very deep and elemental feelings about our own strength.

Still, we Americans want a more humane and stable world. We believe in good will and fairness, as well as strength. This agreement with Panama is something we want because we know it is right. This is not merely the surest way to protect and save the canal, it's a strong, positive act of a people who are still confident, still creative, still great.

This new partnership can become a source of national pride and self-respect in much the same way that building the canal was 75 years ago. It's the spirit in which we act that is so very important.

Theodore Roosevelt, who was President when America built the canal, saw history itself as a force, and the history of our own time and the changes it has brought would not be lost on him. He knew that change was inevitable and necessary. Change is growth. The true conservative, he once remarked, keeps his face to the future.

But if Theodore Roosevelt were to endorse the treaties, as I'm quite sure he would, it would mainly be because he could see the decision as one by which we are demonstrating the kind of great power we wish to be.

"We cannot avoid meeting great issues," Roosevelt said. "All that we can determine for ourselves is whether we shall meet them well or ill."

The Panama Canal is a vast, heroic expression of that age-old desire to bridge the divide and to bring people closer together. This is what the treaties are all about.

We can sense what Roosevelt called "the lift toward nobler things which marks a great and generous people."

In this historic decision, he would join us in our pride for being a great and generous people, with the national strength and wisdom to do what is right for us and what is fair to others.

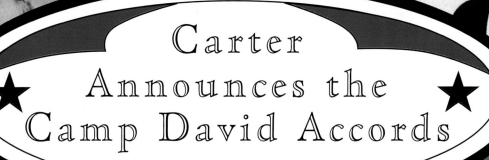

Carter Announces the Camp David Accords

President Carter's most impressive foreign policy achievement was his role in bringing about the signing of a peace treaty between Egypt and Israel. The two countries had been alienated since the establishment of the state of Israel in 1948, and were still technically at war since 1973. In September 1978, Carter brought Egypt's President Anwar Sadat and Israel's Prime Minister Menachem Begin together at the presidential retreat at Camp David in Maryland. During thirteen days of negotiations, the talks broke down more than once. But Carter persisted until the two leaders reached an agreement. On September 17, 1978, Carter announced that a framework for peace had been reached. The following spring, the president visited both Cairo and Tel Aviv to sustain the initiative. On March 26, 1979, on the lawn of the White House, the three leaders signed the treaty, the first ever between Israel and an Arab nation.

When we first arrived at Camp David, the first thing upon which we agreed was to ask the people of the world to pray that our negotiations would be successful. Those prayers have been answered far beyond any expectations. We are privileged to witness tonight a significant achievement in the cause of peace, an achievement none thought possible a year ago, or even a month ago, an achievement that reflects the courage and wisdom of these two leaders.

Through 13 long days at Camp David, we have seen them display determination and vision and flexibility which was needed to make this agreement come to pass. All of us owe them our gratitude and respect. They know that they will always have my personal admiration.

There are still great difficulties that remain and many hard issues to be settled. The questions that have brought warfare and bitterness to the Middle East for the last 30 years will not be settled overnight. But we should all recognize the substantial achievements that have been made.

One of the agreements that President Sadat and Prime Minister Begin are signing tonight is entitled, "A Framework For Peace in the Middle East."

This framework concerns the principles and some specifics in the most substantive way which will govern a comprehensive peace settlement. It deals specifically with the future of the West Bank and Gaza, and the need to resolve the Palestinian problem in all its aspects. The framework document proposes a five-year transitional period in the West Bank and Gaza during which the Israeli military government will be withdrawn and a self-governing authority will be elected with full autonomy.

It also provides for Israeli forces to remain in specified locations during this period to protect Israel's security.

The Palestinians will have the right to participate in the determination of their own future, in negotiations which will resolve the final status of the West Bank and Gaza, and then to produce an Israeli-Jordanian peace treaty.

These negotiations will be based on all the provisions and all the principles of the United Nations Security Council Resolution 242. And it provides that Israel may live in peace within secure and recognized borders.

This great aspiration of Israel has been certified without constraint with the greatest degree of enthusiasm by President Sadat, the leader of one of the greatest nations on earth.

The other document is entitled, "Framework For the Conclusion of a Peace Treaty," between Egypt and Israel.

It provides for the full exercise of Egyptian sovereignty over the Sinai. It calls for the full withdrawal of Israeli forces from the Sinai; and after an interim withdrawal which will be accomplished very quickly, the establishment of normal, peaceful relations between the two countries, including diplomatic relations.

Together with accompanying letters, which we will make public tomorrow, these two Camp David agreements provide the basis for progress and peace throughout the Middle East.

There is one issue on which agreement has not been reached. Egypt states that the agreement to remove Israeli settlements from Egyptian territory is a prerequisite to a peace treaty. Israel states that the issue of Israeli settlements should be resolved during the peace negotiations. That is a substantial difference.

Within the next two weeks, the Knesset [Israel's parliament] will decide on the issue of these settlements.

Tomorrow night, I will go before the Congress to explain these agreements more fully, and to talk about their implications for the United States, and for the world. For the moment, and in closing, I want to speak more personally about my admiration for all those who have taken part in this process, and my hope that the promise of this moment will be fulfilled.

During the last two weeks the members of all three delegations have spent endless hours, day and night, talking, negotiating, grappling with problems that have divided their people for 30 years. Whenever there was a danger that human energy would fail, or patience would be exhausted, or good will would run out—and there were such moments—these two leaders and the able advisers in all delegations found the resources within them to keep the chances for peace alive.

Well, the long days at Camp David are over. But many months of difficult negotiations still lie ahead.

I hope that the foresight and the wisdom that have made this session a success will guide these leaders and the leaders of all nations as they continue the process toward peace.

Thank you very much.

"Crisis of Confidence" Speech

By mid-1979, the Carter administration was faced with a national sense of crisis, in part because of a worsening economy (particularly the severe gasoline shortages and high increases in oil prices) and in part the result of a growing public perception of presidential ineptitude in dealing with this and other problems facing the nation. The President had postponed an address to the nation planned for delivery after the Organization of Petroleum Exporting Countries (OPEC) announced its fourth, and largest, price increase in five months. Instead, he spoke on July 15, 1979, after having met with dozens of Americans from all walks of life. He subordinated the energy crisis to the "crisis of confidence," which, he maintained, was the country's most pressing problem.

Carter's speech was well received. Yet, just a few days later, the president undermined his own message by accepting the forced resignations of five members of his cabinet. This purge of the cabinet made it appear that Carter's administration was falling apart, further eroding public confidence in the president's leadership.

Good evening.

This is a special night for me. Exactly 3 years ago, on July 15, 1976, I accepted the nomination of my party to run for President of the United States.

I promised you a President who is not isolated from the people, who feels your pain, and who shares your dreams and who draws his strength and his wisdom from you.

During the past 3 years I've spoken to you on many occasions about national concerns, the energy crisis, reorganizing the Government, our Nation's economy, and issues of war and especially peace. But over those years the subjects of the speeches, the talks, and the press conferences have become increasingly narrow focused more and more on what the isolated world of Washington thinks is important. Gradually, you've heard more and more about what the Government thinks or what the Government should be doing and less and less about our Nation's hopes, our dreams, and our vision of the future.

Ten days ago I had planned to speak to you again about a very important subject—energy. For the fifth time I would have described the urgency of the problem and laid out a series of legislative recommendations to the Congress. But as I was preparing to speak, I began to ask myself the same question that I now know has been troubling many of you. Why have we not been able to get together as a nation to resolve our serious energy problem?

It's clear that the true problems of our Nation are much deeper—deeper than gasoline lines or energy shortages, deeper even than inflation or recession. And I realize more than ever that as President I need your help. So, I decided to reach out and listen to the voices of America.

I invited to Camp David people from almost every segment of our society—business and labor, teachers and preachers, Governors, mayors, and private citizens. And then I left Camp David to listen to other Americans, men and women like you.

It has been an extraordinary 10 days, and I want to share with you what I've heard. First of all, I got a lot of personal advice. Let me quote a few of the typical comments that I wrote down.

This from a southern Governor: "Mr. President, you are not leading this Nation—you're just managing the Government."

"You don't see the people enough any more."

"Some of your Cabinet members don't seem loyal. There is not enough discipline among your disciples."

"Don't talk to us about politics or the mechanics of government, but about an understanding of our common good."

"Mr. President, we're in trouble. Talk to us about blood and sweat and tears."

"If you lead, Mr. President, we will follow."

Many people talked about themselves and about the condition of our Nation. This from a young woman in Pennsylvania: "I feel so far from government. I feel like ordinary people are excluded from political power."

And this from a young Chicano: "Some of us have suffered from recession all our lives."

"Some people have wasted energy, but others haven't had anything to waste."

And this from a religious leader: "No material shortage can touch the important things like God's love for us or our love for one another."

And I like this one particularly from a black woman who happens to be the mayor of a small Mississippi town: "The big-shots are not the only ones who are important. Remember, you can't sell anything on Wall Street unless someone digs it up somewhere else first."

This kind of summarized a lot of other statements: "Mr. President, we are confronted with a moral and a spiritual crisis." [. . .]

These 10 days confirmed my belief in the decency and the strength and the wisdom of the American people, but it also bore out some of my long-standing concerns about our Nation's underlying problems.

I know, of course, being President, that government actions and legislation can be very important. That's why I've worked hard to put my campaign promises into law—and I have to admit, with just mixed success. But after listening to the American people I have been reminded again that all the legislation in the world can't fix what's wrong with America. So, I want to speak to you first tonight about a subject even more serious than energy or inflation. I want to talk to you right now about a fundamental threat to American democracy.

I do not mean our political and civil liberties. They will endure. And I do not refer to the outward strength of America, a nation that is at peace tonight everywhere in the world, with unmatched economic power and military might.

The threat is nearly invisible in ordinary ways. It is a crisis of confidence. It is a crisis that strikes at the very heart and soul and spirit of our national will. We can see this crisis in the growing doubt about the meaning of our own lives and in the loss of a unity of purpose for our Nation.

The erosion of our confidence in the future is threatening to destroy the social and the political fabric of America.

The confidence that we have always had as a people is not simply some romantic dream or a proverb in a dusty book that we read just on the Fourth of July.

It is the idea which founded our Nation and has guided our development as a people. Confidence in the future has supported everything else—public institutions and private enterprise, our own families, and the very Constitution of the United States. Confidence has defined our course and has served as a link between generations. We've always believed in something called progress. We've always had a faith that the days of our children would be better than our own.

Our people are losing that faith, not only in government itself but in the ability as citizens to serve as the ultimate rulers and shapers of our democracy. As a people we know our past and we are proud of it. Our progress has been part of the living history of America, even the world. We always believed that we were part of a great movement of humanity itself called democracy, involved in the search for freedom, and that belief has always strengthened us in our purpose. But just as we are losing our confidence in the future, we are also beginning to close the door on our past.

In a nation that was proud of hard work, strong families, close-knit communities, and our faith in God, too many of us now tend to worship self-indulgence and consumption. Human identity is no longer defined by what one does, but by what one owns. But we've discovered that owning things and consuming things does not satisfy our longing for meaning. We've learned that piling up material goods cannot fill the emptiness of lives which have no confidence or purpose.

The symptoms of this crisis of the American spirit are all around us. For the first time in the history of our country a majority of our people believe that the next five years will be worse than the past five years. Two-thirds of our people do not even vote. The productivity of American workers is actually dropping, and the willingness of Americans to save for the future has fallen below that of all other people in the Western world.

As you know, there is a growing disrespect for government and for churches and for schools, the news media, and other institutions. This is not a message of happiness or reassurance, but it is the truth and it is a warning.

These changes did not happen overnight. They've come upon us gradually over the last generation, years that were filled with shocks and tragedy.

We were sure that ours was a nation of the ballot, not the bullet, until the murders of John Kennedy and Robert Kennedy and Martin Luther King, Jr. We were taught that our armies were always invincible and our causes were always just, only to suffer the agony of Vietnam. We respected the Presidency as a place of honor until the shock of Watergate.

Selection of Carter items. The federal election law of 1974 limited expenditures by presidential candidates. Paradoxically, independent political action committees (PACs) proliferated. Therefore, the issuance of many campaign items shifted from central committees to PACs.

TONY RUFFINO, LARRY VAUGHN & DON LAW
present

THE ALLMAN BROTHERS BAND

IN A BENEFIT CONCERT FOR

Jimmy Carter
Democratic Presidential Candidate

TUES. NOVEMBER 25 at 8 P.M.
PROVIDENCE CIVIC CENTER

Tickets $6.50 Advance $7.50 Day of Show

PAID FOR BY THE COMMITTEE FOR JIMMY CARTER, R.J. LIPSHULTZ—TREAS.
TICKET PURCHASE IS A CONTRIBUTION TO THE JIMMY CARTER PRESIDENTIAL CAMPAIGN.

A COPY OF OUR REPORT IS FILED WITH THE FEDERAL ELECTION COMMISSION, WASHINGTON, D.C.

THE NEXT PRESIDENT OF THE U·S·A· 1976

JIMMY CARTER

We remember when the phrase "sound as a dollar" was an expression of absolute dependability, until 10 years of inflation began to shrink our dollar and our savings. We believed that our Nation's resources were limitless until 1973, when we had to face a growing dependence on foreign oil.

These wounds are still very deep. They have never been healed. Looking for a way out of this crisis, our people have turned to the Federal Government and found it isolated from the mainstream of our Nation's life. Washington,

 105

D.C., has become an island. The gap between our citizens and our Government has never been so wide. The people are looking for honest answers, not easy answers; clear leadership, not false claims and evasiveness and politics as usual.

What you see too often in Washington and elsewhere around the country is a system of government that seems incapable of action. You see a Congress twisted and pulled in every direction by hundreds of well-financed and powerful special interests. You see every extreme position defended to the last vote, almost to the last breath by one unyielding group or another. You often see a balanced and a fair approach that demands sacrifice, a little sacrifice from everyone, abandoned like an orphan without support and without friends.

Often you see paralysis and stagnation and drift. You don't like it, and neither do I. What can we do?

First of all, we must face the truth, and then we can change our course. We simply must have faith in each other, faith in our ability to govern ourselves, and faith in the future of this Nation. Restoring that faith and that confidence to America is now the most important task we face. It is a true challenge of this generation of Americans.

One of the visitors to Camp David last week put it this way: "We've got to stop crying and start sweating, stop talking and start walking, stop cursing and start praying. The strength we need will not come from the White House, but from every house in America."

We know the strength of America. We are strong. We can regain our unity. We can regain our confidence. We are the heirs of generations who survived threats much more powerful and awesome than those that challenge

Button showing support for Carter.

us now. Our fathers and mothers were strong men and women who shaped a new society during the Great Depression, who fought world wars, and who carved out a new charter of peace for the world.

We ourselves are the same Americans who just 10 years ago put a man on the Moon. We are the generation that dedicated our society to the pursuit of human rights and equality. And we are the generation that will win the war on the energy problem and in that process rebuild the unity and confidence of America. [. . .]

Little by little we can and we must rebuild our confidence. We can spend until we empty our treasuries, and we may summon all the wonders of science. But we can succeed only if we tap our greatest resources—America's people, America's values, and America's confidence.

I have seen the strength of America in the inexhaustible resources of our people. In the days to come, let us renew that strength in the struggle for an energy secure nation.

In closing, let me say this: I will do my best, but I will not do it alone. Let your voice be heard. Whenever you have a chance, say something good about our country. With God's help and for the sake of our Nation, it is time for us to join hands in America. Let us commit ourselves together to a rebirth of the American spirit. Working together with our common faith we cannot fail.

Thank you and good night.

Failure of the Hostage Rescue Mission

If Carter's greatest foreign policy triumph involved the Middle East, so did his greatest failure—the collapse of American relations with Iran. The seemingly endless Iranian hostage crisis dominated the last year of the Carter presidency and seriously impaired his chances for re-election in 1980. Fifty-two Americans, seized by Ayatollah Ruhollah Khomeini's Revolutionary Guards on November 4, 1979, spent 444 days in captivity. They returned home in January 1981, shortly after Ronald Reagan entered the White House. The Iranian militants, committed to a form of Islam that rejects modernization, associated the United States with Mohammad Reza Pahlavi, the Shah of Iran who had been overthrown by Khomeini's movement. Diplomacy failed to alter the hostage situation.

On April 25, 1980, with Carter's authorization, 130 men from the elite U.S. Army Special Forces deployed in a remote salt desert site 265 miles southeast of Teheran. Almost immediately, the raid commander decided to abort the mission because of the malfunctioning of three helicopters. In their haste to depart, a maneuvering helicopter struck a supply airplane, engulfing both craft in flames. Eight men died. This disheartening setback also resulted in the resignation of Secretary of State Cyrus Vance, who opposed using military force to deal with the hostage crisis. The next morning, a somber President Carter addressed the nation.

Late yesterday, I cancelled a carefully planned operation which was underway in Iran to position our rescue team for later withdrawal of American hostages, who have been held captive there since 4 November. Equipment failure in the rescue helicopters made it necessary to end the mission.

As our team was withdrawing, after my order to do so, two of our American aircraft collided on the ground following a refueling operation in a remote desert location in Iran. Other information about this rescue mission will be made available to the American people when it is appropriate to do so.

There was no fighting; there was no combat. But to my deep regret, eight of the crewmen of the two aircraft which collided were killed, and several other Americans were hurt in the incident. Our people were immediately airlifted from Iran. Those who were injured have gotten medical treatment, and all of them are expected to recover.

No knowledge of this operation by any Iranian officials or authorities was evident to us until several hours after all Americans were withdrawn from Iran.

Our rescue team knew and I knew that the operation was certain to be difficult and it was certain to be dangerous. We were all convinced that if and when the rescue operation had been commenced that it had an excellent chance of success. They were all volunteers; they were all highly trained. I met with their leaders before they went on this operation. They knew then what hopes of mine and of all Americans they carried with them.

To the families of those who died and who were wounded, I want to express the admiration I feel for the courage of their loved ones and the sorrow that I feel personally for their sacrifice.

The mission on which they were embarked was a humanitarian

mission. It was not directed against Iran; it was not directed against the people of Iran. It was not undertaken with any feeling of hostility toward Iran or its people. It has caused no Iranian casualties.

Planning for this rescue effort began shortly after our Embassy was seized, but for a number of reasons, I waited until now to put those rescue plans into effect. To be feasible, this complex operation had to be the product of intensive planning and intensive training and repeated rehearsal. However, a resolution of this crisis through negotiations and with voluntary action on the part of the Iranian officials was obviously then, has been, and will be preferable.

This rescue attempt had to await my judgment that the Iranian authorities could not or would not resolve this crisis on their own initiative. With the steady unraveling of authority in Iran and the mounting dangers that were posed to the safety of the hostages themselves and the growing realization that their early release was highly unlikely, I made a decision to commence the rescue operations plans.

This attempt became a necessity and a duty. The readiness of our team to undertake the rescue made it completely practicable. Accordingly, I made the decision to set our long-developed plans into operation. I ordered this rescue mission prepared in order to safeguard American lives, to protect America's national interests, and to reduce the tensions in the world that have been caused among many nations as this crisis has continued.

It was my decision to attempt the rescue operation. It was my decision to cancel it when problems developed in the placement of our rescue team for a future rescue operation. The responsibility is fully my own.

In the aftermath of the attempt, we continue to hold the Government of Iran responsible for the safety and for the early release of the American hostages who have been held so long. The United States remains determined to bring about their safe release at the earliest date possible.

As President, I know that our entire Nation feels the deep gratitude I feel for the brave men who were prepared to rescue their fellow Americans from captivity. And as President, I also know that the Nation shares not only my disappointment that the rescue effort could not be mounted, because of mechanical difficulties, but also my determination to persevere and to bring all of our hostages home to freedom.

We have been disappointed before. We will not give up in our efforts. Throughout this extraordinarily difficult period, we have pursued and will continue to pursue every possible avenue to secure the release of the hostages. In these efforts, the support of the American people and of our friends throughout the world has been a most crucial element. That support of other nations is even more important now.

We will seek to continue, along with other nations and with the officials of Iran, a prompt resolution of the crisis without any loss of life and through peaceful and diplomatic means.

★ President Carter's ★ Farewell Address

During the 1980 presidential campaign, Ronald Reagan and Jimmy Carter had very different campaign themes. Reagan successfully exploited domestic distress and international instability. He promised to restore America to greatness. He promised the American people an America like that of his youth, rooted in what he called small-town, rural values: patriotism, self-help, hard work, morality, and belief in God, family, and the flag. On the other hand, Carter repeated that America had to sacrifice in order to survive in a world of scarcity. Carter tried to divert attention from his own record by emphasizing Reagan's right-wing background. He warned that Reagan's election would be a threat to peace. During the second television debate with Carter, Reagan scored the most decisive point in the campaign. He ended the debate with two brilliant questions: "Ask yourself, are you better off than you were four years ago?" and "Is America as respected throughout the world as it was four years ago?" "The election," said a Carter adviser, "ended up becoming exactly the referendum on unhappiness we had been trying to avoid."

On January 14, 1981, six days before president-elect Reagan's inauguration, Carter delivered this farewell address.

Good evening. In a few days, I will lay down my official responsibilities in this office—to take up once more the only title in our democracy superior to that of president, the title of citizen.

Of Vice President Mondale, my Cabinet and the hundreds of others who have served with me during the last four years, I wish to say publicly what I have said in private: I thank them for the dedication and competence they have brought to the service of our country.

But I owe my deepest thanks to you, the American people, because you gave me this extraordinary opportunity to serve. We have faced great challenges together. We know that future problems will also be difficult, but I am now more convinced than ever that the United States—better than any other nation—can meet successfully whatever the future might bring.

These last four years have made me more certain than ever of the inner strength of our country—the unchanging value of our principles and ideals, the stability of our political system, the ingenuity and the decency of our people.

Tonight I would like first to say a few words about this most special office, the presidency of the United States.

This is at once the most powerful office in the world—and among the most severely constrained by law and custom. The president is given a broad responsibility to lead—but cannot do so without the support and consent of the people, expressed informally through the Congress and informally in many ways through a whole range of public and private institutions.

This is as it should be. Within our system of government every American has a right and duty to help shape the future course of the United States.

Thoughtful criticism and close scrutiny of all government officials by the press and the public are an important part of our democratic society. Now as in our past, only the understanding and involvement of the people through full and open debate can help to avoid serious mistakes and assure the continued dignity and safety of the nation.

Today we are asking our political system to do things of which the founding fathers never dreamed. The government they designed for a few hundred thousand people now serves a nation of almost 230 million people. Their small coastal republic now spans beyond a continent, and we now have the responsibility to help lead much of the world through difficult times to a secure and prosperous future.

Today, as people have become ever more doubtful of the ability of the government to deal with our problems, we are increasingly drawn to single-issue groups and special interest organizations to ensure that whatever else happens our own personal views and our own private interests are protected.

This is a disturbing factor in American political life. It tends to distort our purposes because the national interest is not always the sum of all our single or special interests. We are all Americans together—and we must not forget that the common good is our common interest and our individual responsibility.

Because of the fragmented pressures of special interests, it's very important that the office of the president be a strong one, and that its constitutional authority be preserved. The president is the only elected official charged with the primary responsibility of representing all the people. In the moments of decision, after the different and conflicting views have been aired, it is the president who then must speak to the nation and for the nation.

I understand after four years in office, as few others can, how formidable is the task the president-elect is about to undertake. To the very limits of conscience and conviction, I pledge to support him in that task. I wish him success, and Godspeed.

I know from experience that presidents have to face major issues that are controversial, broad in scope, and which do not arouse the natural support of a political majority.

For a few minutes now, I want to lay aside my role as leader of one nation, and speak to you as a fellow citizen of the world about three issues, three difficult issues: The threat of nuclear destruction, our stewardship of the physical resources of our planet, and the pre-eminence of the basic rights of human beings.

It's now been 35 years since the first atomic bomb fell on Hiroshima. The great majority of the world's people cannot remember a time when the nuclear shadow did not hang over the earth. Our minds have adjusted to it, as after a time our eyes adjust to the dark.

Yet the risk of a nuclear conflagration has not lessened. It has not happened yet, thank God, but that can give us little comfort—for it only has to happen once.

The danger is becoming greater. As the arsenals of the superpowers grow in size and sophistication and as other governments acquire these weapons, it may only be a matter of time before madness, desperation, greed or miscalculation lets lose this terrible force.

In an all-out nuclear war, more destructive power than in all of World War II would be unleashed every second during the long afternoon it would take for all the missiles and bombs to fall. A World War II every second—more people killed in the first few hours than all the wars of history put together. The survivors, if any, would live in despair amid the poisoned ruins of a civilization that had committed suicide.

National weakness—real or perceived—can tempt aggression and thus cause war. That's why the United States cannot neglect its military strength. We must and we will remain strong. But with equal determination, the United States and all countries must find ways to control and reduce the horrifying danger that is posed by the world's enormous stockpiles of nuclear arms.

This has been a concern of every American president since the moment we first saw what these weapons could do. Our leaders will require our understanding and our support as they grapple with this difficult but crucial challenge. There is no disagreement on the goals or the basic approach to controlling this enormous destructive force. The answer lies not just in the attitudes or actions of world leaders, but in the concern and demands of all of us as we continue our struggle to preserve the peace.

Nuclear weapons are an expression of one side of our human character. But there is another side. The same rocket technology that delivers nuclear warheads has also taken us peacefully into space. From that perspective, we see our Earth as it really is—a small and fragile and beautiful blue globe, the only home we have. We see no barriers of race or religion or country. We see the essential unity of our species and our planet; and with faith and common sense, that bright vision will ultimately prevail.

Another major challenge, therefore, is to protect the quality of this world within which we live. The shadows that fail across the future are cast not only by the kinds of weapons we have built, but by the kind of world we will either nourish or neglect.

There are real and growing dangers to our simple and most precious possessions: the air we breathe; the water we drink; and the land which sustain us. The rapid depletion of irreplaceable minerals, the erosion of top-soil, the destruction of beauty, the blight of pollution, the demands of increasing billions of people, all combine to create problems which are easy to observe and predict but difficult to resolve. If we do not act, the world of the year 2000 will be much less able to sustain life than it is now.

But there is no reason for despair. Acknowledging the physical realities of our planet does not mean a dismal future of endless sacrifice. In fact, acknowledging these realities is the first step in dealing with them. We can meet the resource problems of the world—water, food, minerals, farmlands, forests, overpopulation, pollution—if we tackle them with courage and foresight.

I have just been talking about forces of potential destruction that mankind has developed, and how we might control them. It is equally important that we remember the beneficial forces that we have evolved over the ages, and how to hold fast to them.

One of those constructive forces is enhancement of individual human freedoms through the strengthening of democracy, and the fight against deprivation, torture, terrorism and the persecution of people throughout the world. The struggle for human rights overrides all differences of color, nation or language.

Those who hunger for freedom, who thirst for human dignity, and who suffer for the sake of justice—they are the patriots of this cause.

I believe with all my heart that America must always stand for these basic human rights—at home and abroad. That is both our history and our destiny.

America did not invent human rights. In a very real sense, it is the other way round. Human rights invented America.

Ours was the first nation in the history of the world to be founded explicitly on such an idea. Our social and political progress has been based on one fundamental principle—the value and importance of the individual. The fundamental force that unites us is not kinship or place of origin or religious preference. The love of liberty is a common blood that flows in our American veins.

The battle for human rights—at home and abroad—is far from over. We should never be surprised nor discouraged because the impact of our efforts has had, and will always have, varied results. Rather, we should take pride that the ideals which gave birth to our nation still inspire the hopes of oppressed people around the world. We have no cause for self-righteousness or complacency. But we have every reason to persevere, both within our own country and beyond our borders.

If we are to serve as a beacon for human rights, we must continue to perfect here at home the rights and values which we espouse around the world: A decent education for our children, adequate medical care for all Americans, an end to discrimination against minorities and women, a job for all those able to work, and freedom from injustice and religious intolerance.

Re-Elect
Carter-Mondale

A Tested and Trustworthy Team.

Carter-Mondale campaign poster from the 1980 election. Ronald Reagan won 50.7 percent of the national vote while Carter received 41 percent. Third-party candidate John Anderson finished with about 6.6 percent.

We live in a time of transition, an uneasy era which is likely to endure for the rest of this century. It will be a period of tensions both within nations and between nations—of competition for scarce resources, of social political and economic stresses and strains. During this period we may be tempted to abandon some of the time-honored principles and commitments which have been proven during the difficult times of past generations.

We must never yield to this temptation. Our American values are not luxuries but necessities—not the salt in our bread but the bread itself. Our common vision of a free and just society is our greatest source of cohesion at home and strength abroad—greater even than the bounty of our material blessings.

Remember these words:

"We hold these truths to be self-evident, that all men are created equal; that they are endowed by their creator with certain inalienable rights; that among these are life liberty and the pursuit of happiness."

This vision still grips the imagination of the world. But we know that democracy is always an unfinished creation. Each generation must renew its foundations. Each generation must rediscover the meaning of this hallowed vision in the light of its own modern challenges. For this generation, ours, life is nuclear survival; liberty is human rights; the pursuit of happiness is a planet whose resources are devoted to the physical and spiritual nourishment of its inhabitants.

During the next few days I will work hard to make sure that the transition from myself to the next president is a good one so that the American people are served well. And I will continue as I have the last 14 months to work hard and to pray for the lives and the well-being of the American hostages held in Iran. I can't predict yet what will happen, but I hope you will join me in my constant prayer for their freedom.

As I return home to the South where I was born and raised, I am looking forward to the opportunity to reflect and further to assess—I hope with accuracy—the circumstances of our times. I intend to give our new president my support, and I intend to work as a citizen, as I have worked in this office as president, for the values this nation was founded to secure.

Again, from the bottom of my heart, I want to express to you the gratitude I feel.

Thank you, fellow citizens, and farewell.

Further Reading

GENERAL REFERENCE

Israel, Fred L. *Student's Atlas of American Presidential Elections, 1789–1996*. Washington, D.C.: Congressional Quarterly Books, 1998.

Levy, Peter B., editor. *100 Key Documents in American History*. Westport, Conn.: Praeger, 1999.

Mieczkowski, Yarek. *The Routledge Historical Atlas of Presidential Elections*. New York: Routledge, 2001.

Polsby, Nelson W., and Aaron Wildavsky. *Presidential Elections: Strategies and Structures of American Politics*. 10th edition. New York: Chatham House, 2000.

Watts, J. F., and Fred L. Israel, editors. *Presidential Documents*. New York: Routledge, 2000.

Widmer, Ted. *The New York Times Campaigns: A Century of Presidential Races*. New York: DK Publishing, 2000.

POLITICAL AMERICANA REFERENCE

Cunningham, Noble E. Jr. *Popular Images of the Presidency: From Washington to Lincoln*. Columbia: University of Missouri Press, 1991.

Melder, Keith. *Hail to the Candidate: Presidential Campaigns from Banners to Broadcasts*. Washington, D.C.: Smithsonian Institution Press, 1992.

Schlesinger, Arthur M. jr., Fred L. Israel, and David J. Frent. *Running for President: The Candidates and their Images*. 2 vols. New York: Simon and Schuster, 1994.

Warda, Mark. *100 Years of Political Campaign Collectibles*. Clearwater, Fla.: Galt Press, 1996.

THE ELECTION OF 1976
And the Administration of Jimmy Carter

Anderson, Patrick. *Electing Jimmy Carter: The Campaign of 1976*. Baton Rouge: Louisiana State University Press, 1994.

Bourne, Peter G. *Jimmy Carter: A Comprehensive Biography from Plains to Post-Presidency*. New York: Scribner, 1997.

Brinkley, Douglas. *The Unfinished Presidency: Jimmy Carter's Journey Beyond the White House*. New York: Viking Press, 1998.

Cannon, James M. *Time and Chance: Gerald Ford's Appointment With History*. Ann Arbor: University of Michigan Press, 1998.

Carter, Jimmy. *Keeping Faith: Memoirs of a President*. New York: Bantam Doubleday Dell, 1982.

Fink, Gary M., and Hugh Davis Graham, editors. *The Carter Presidency: Policy Choices in the Post-New Deal Era*. Lawrence: University Press of Kansas, 1998.

Germond, Jack. *Blue Smoke and Mirrors: How Reagan Won and Why Carter Lost the Election of 1980*. New York: Viking Press, 1981.

Greene, John Robert. *The Presidency of Gerald R. Ford*. Lawrence: University Press of Kansas, 1995.

Grover, William F. *The President as Prisoner: A Structural Critique of the Carter and Reagan Years*. Albany: State University of New York Press, 1989.

Kaufman, Burton I. *The Presidency of James Earl Carter Jr.* Lawrence: University Press of Kansas, 1993.

Rosenbaum, Herbert D., and Alexei Ugrinsky, editors. *Jimmy Carter: Foreign Policy and Post-Presidential Years*. Westport, Conn.: Greenwood Publishing Group, 1994.

Witcover, Jules. *Marathon: The Pursuit of the Presidency, 1972–1976*. New York: Viking Press, 1977.

INDEX

Numbers in **bold italics** refer to captions.

The ★ EDITORS ★

ARTHUR M. SCHLESINGER JR. holds the Albert Schweitzer Chair in the Humanities at the Graduate Center of the City University of New York. He is the author of more than a dozen books, including *The Age of Jackson*; *The Vital Center; The Age of Roosevelt* (3 vols.); *A Thousand Days: John F. Kennedy in the White House; Robert Kennedy and His Times; The Cycles of American History;* and *The Imperial Presidency*. Professor Schlesinger served as Special Assistant to President Kennedy (1961–63). His numerous awards include: the Pulitzer Prize for History; the Pulitzer Prize for Biography; two National Book Awards; The Bancroft Prize; and the American Academy of Arts and Letters Gold Medal for History.

FRED L. ISRAEL is professor emeritus of American history, City College of New York. He is the author of *Nevada's Key Pittman* and has edited *The War Diary of Breckinridge Long* and *Major Peace Treaties of Modern History, 1648–1975* (5 vols.) He holds the Scribe's Award from the American Bar Association for his joint editorship of the *Justices of the United States Supreme Court* (4 vols.). For more than 25 years Professor Israel has compiled and edited the Gallup Poll into annual reference volumes.

DAVID J. FRENT is the president of Political Americana Auctions, Oakhurst, NJ. With his wife, Janice, he has assembled the nation's foremost private collection of political campaign memorabilia. Mr. Frent has designed exhibits for corporations, the Smithsonian Institution, and the United States Information Agency. A member of the board of directors of the American Political Items Collectors since 1972, he was elected to its Hall of Fame for his "outstanding contribution to preserving and studying our political heritage."